Hidden Treasures

A collection of original drama pieces

Pip Parry

compiled and edited by Christina Lay

© Pip Parry 1999

First published 2003

Edition 1.1

ISBN 0–9545180–0–4

Compiled, keyed and edited by Christina Lay

Cover design by Harry Edwards

Published by Parrilay Plays, MK

Printed by Grillford Limited, Milton Keynes

Acknowledgements

Grateful thanks are due to:

all members of Third-Age Players for their support while this project was under way;
Harry Edwards for cover design and printing advice;
Jeffery Lay and Stephanie Gray for Website design;
Mrs Jackie Jones, Cy Pearson, Vera Roper, Jocelyn Lord, Thelma Billington, John Fone, Phyllis Parry and Roy Hooley, for permission to use photos.

Applications for performing rights may be made directly to the Author and addressed as follows:

Parrilay Plays, c/o Pip Parry, 17 Lissel Road, Simpson, Milton Keynes. MK6

A Performing Rights Application Form is supplied in the end pages of this book. Please reply to all questions. Alternatively, apply on website:

www.Parrilay.co.uk

Contents

---

* This item contains titles or references that are specific to the Milton Keynes area. It is possible to make appropriate substitutions in order to relate to performance elsewhere. The Publishers will be glad to be informed or to be approached for guidance.

Part 4: Playlets and one-acts

Appendix: items written especially for Third-Age performers

---

* This item contains titles or references that are specific to the Milton Keynes area. It is possible to make appropriate substitutions in order to relate to performance elsewhere. The Publishers will be glad to be informed or to be approached for guidance.

Editor's Foreword

I had known Pip Parry for a few years as a fellow actor in the Open Theatre Group (based at the Open University) and knew him also to belong to U3A, the University of the Third Age, the international leisure and self-development organisation for retired people. In 1997 the local U3A magazine contained an invitation from Pip to help form a drama group within the Milton Keynes U3A. I was among the dozen or so who responded.

When the inaugural group met we were amazed and grateful to see the selection of original material Pip revealed, from which we compiled a programme for our first Revue. During the ensuing years he has gradually revealed a treasury of material dating back many years, some of which had been performed by other drama groups. At the date of writing (1999), though he is now 78 years of age, new material is still constantly emerging. He long remained resistant to the urging of his Directors and actors to publish. This volume is therefore the result of a (benign) conspiracy within the group to get the material keyed, compiled and edited. We have finally managed to persuade Pip to let us go ahead and to supply the date and history of each piece.

We are confident that future readers and performers will derive as much delight from this material as we have.

Christina Lay, Editor, 1999–2003
on behalf of the members of **Milton Keynes Third-Age Players**

Notes on Performance

Please complete and return the Application form if you intend to perform any of the items in this book. The project has not been undertaken for profit, and genuine amateur or Charity performances will be assessed at a minimal or zero rate, provided adequate credits are assured.

Author's Foreword

How did I get into all this?

My hitherto unsung career as a script-writer began, I think, during my last year in primary school, when an eccentric teacher used our daily arithmetic periods to encourage us to improvise and act out our own playlets. As a result I developed an abiding interest in things theatrical and an abiding weakness in mathematics. I was probably lucky to scrape my Maths 'O' level. In my 'teens I wrote sketches, now mercifully forgotten, for a Youth Club concert-party.

In the 1970s and early '80s, as a member of a newly formed drama group in Caversham Park Village (a newly developed housing area near Reading) I found myself cast as resident scriptwriter to the pretentiously named Caversham Park Theatre. By now I was turning out revue sketches, some of which appear in the following pages, and a number of full-length offerings, mainly offbeat versions of familiar pantomimes, which were performed in the lovely little Kenton theatre in Henley-on-Thames.

Even now, long retired from gainful work, and a member of the Third-Age Players (TAP) here in Milton Keynes, I have not yet been able to kick the habit. My addiction is aided and abetted, I must acknowledge, by the rest of the TAP group. Even though what I produce is intended only to raise a few chuckles, nowadays I find it harder to write. I never found it easy. For me, it requires listening to other people's conversation, scribbling surreptitious notes, writing and rewriting several times, and ending up with a two-finger assault on an ageing typewriter. My own favourite 'creation', which, for obvious reasons, cannot be performed by TAP, is a version of *Babes in the Wood*, featuring the Marx Brothers. It helps, you see, if one is just a little bit barmy.

Pip Parry, 2000.

Part 1
Solos and monologues

Part 1 Solos and monologues

Costume Lady

[First performed in a Caversham Park Theatre (CPT) Revue in 1982; revived for an Open Theatre Group (OTG) Revue in 1990 and for TAP in 1998]

Monologue for female.

The essential setting is a clothing rail in the background, with various costumes, and a box with hats. The Costume Lady is insignificant in appearance, apologetic, speaks with a regional accent in her verses, but becomes surprisingly eloquent and impressive in her quoted passages.

I look after costumes:
That's all they'll let me do.
I'm no kind of an actress:
At least I know that's true.
I don't get even small parts,
It would cause too much alarm.
So they put me on to costumes,
Where I can't do no harm.

But when I'm in our store-room,
I'm let out of a cage!
I try on all those costumes
And I feel I'm on the stage!
I can't play Cinderella,
Finding romance at the ball,
But when I wear her costume,
I'm the greatest of them all!
I'm the greatest Cinderella of them all!

Holding a ragged dress against her, she becomes a sad Cinderella.

Everyone in the Kingdom is invited to the Ball at the Palace. Even me … ! But what use is that? How can I go? In this dress? It's the only one I have. They wouldn't let me past at the door. No, it's no use dreaming. My two step-sisters will go. And I'll be left here, to look after the house … as usual …

While I'm doing wardrobe
I'm in another age!
I try on all my costumes
And I know I'm on the stage!
I'll never play in Shakespeare,
With a Romeo to enthral,
But wearing Juliet's costume,
I'm the greatest of them all!
Yes, I'm the greatest Juliet of them all!

With a suitable costume, she becomes Juliet on the balcony.

O Romeo, Romeo! Wherefore art thou Romeo?
Deny thy father and refuse thy name;
Or, if thou wilt not, be but sworn my love,
And I'll no longer be a Capulet.

I'm meant to do the sewing;
Wouldn't do it for a wage.
But trying on my costumes,
I'm transported to the stage!
A hat like Lady Bracknell's
Makes me feel I'm ten feet tall!
And when I wear her costume
I'm the greatest of them all!
I'm the greatest Lady Bracknell of them all!

Donning a magnificent Victorian hat, she is a formidable Lady Bracknell.

… The line is immaterial. Mr Worthing, I confess I feel somewhat bewildered by what you have just told me. To be born, or at any rate bred, in a hand-bag, whether it had handles or not, seems to me to display a contempt for the ordinary decencies of family life that reminds one of the worst excesses of the French Revolution … .

Fitting zips and patches
Would bore a patient sage,
But when I try on costumes
I think I'm on the stage!
Look at Joan of Arc then:
She didn't shrink or crawl.
So when I wear her costume
I'm the greatest of them all!
Yes, I'm the greatest Saint Joan of them all!

Holding a chain-mail tunic against her, she becomes Joan of Arc.

If you command me to declare that all that I have done and said, and all the visions and revelations I have had, were not from God, then that is impossible: I will not declare it for anything in the world. What God made me do I will never go back on.

> Dressing leading ladies
> Often puts me in a rage,
> But when I try on costumes,
> It's like I'm on the stage!
> Poor Maria Marten!
> See her riding for a fall:
> But when I wear her costume,
> I'm the greatest of them all!
> Yes, I'm the best Maria of them all!

Clutching a shawl, she dies convincingly as Maria.

William, I am dying – your cruel hand has stilled the heart that loved thee. Death claims me – but with my last breath I die blessing and forgiving thee.

She stands.

> There's no harm in dreaming
> Of things that cannot be.
> This is no audition:
> There's no-one here but me …
> As long as no-one's watching,
> I'll take my curtain-call.
> For when I try on costumes,
> I'm the greatest of them all!
> Yes, I'm the greatest actress of them all!

She takes a bow.

SLOW CURTAIN OR BLACKOUT

Lament of the odd-job boy

[Originally written for the part of the odd-job boy, an unlikely
character in Pip's version of *The Sleeping Beauty*, performed by the
Caversham Park Theatre in the 1980s]

I go for a job: they say, 'Make a success of it.'
I don't like the work and I couldn't think less of it.
So it always turns out that I make a big mess of it.
So they make me the odd-job boy.

I try a new job though I'd rather keep clear of it.
They say 'Don't give up', but I tremble for fear of it.
I try it again and I make a pig's ear of it.
So I'm still the odd-job boy.

I do things all wrong and they think Lord-knows-what of me.
I have an idea that they'd like to get shot of me.
How lucky they are that there isn't a lot of me!
I'm the only odd-job boy.

Time passes on: they haven't got rid of me.
I really have tried to do just what was bid of me.
I'm middle-aged now but they still make a kid of me.
I'm still just the odd-job boy.

I make a mistake and my Masters are mad at me.
I do it again and they yell something bad at me.
They finally threaten to let loose my Dad at me.
I'm only the odd-job boy.

Wherever they put me, all jobs are the same to me.
Door-keeper, office-boy, they're all fair game to me.
Oddly enough, though, they can't put a name to me.
I'm always 'the odd-job boy'.

Watching the world go by

[**A monologue for an older actor,** written for TAP's fourth Revue, **Spring Fever,** in May 2000 and performed by Doreen Taylor, but could be performed by any age.]

The lady *is seated at a restaurant table, laid for tea for one.*

I like coming to this restaurant. Just for a cup of tea, mind you. Not anything else. Not for what they charge – I do better at home. ... No, I like to watch the other people. It's like watching the world go by, you might say. You get all sorts in here, as long as they can pay the bill. It's real life, isn't it? I know some people prefer to sit at home and watch soaps. Well, they're welcome to their soaps – but soaps aren't real life, are they?

She takes a sip of tea.

The people here are real. They've all got their problems – you can see it in their faces. ... I've been looking at that lady over there, the one in the grey dress. She looks miserable to me. Wouldn't you say she looks miserable? What age would you say she was – middle-thirties? Perhaps a bit older. Is she married? (she cranes her neck) Well, she's wearing a wedding ring. I wonder why she's on her own? A widow, maybe – or divorced, more likely. Her husband reaches the dangerous age and goes off with some floozie, very likely his secretary. It's so common these days and it makes me cross, I can tell you! There's this man off enjoying himself, while his poor wife – or ex-wife – is left on her own, looking miserable. ... Oho, wait a minute! There's some man joining her. Yes, he's sitting with her. ... But what a drip! Have you ever seen such a drippy-looking man? ... I think she's miserable because he hasn't left her!

She giggles, then looks round.

That waiter's looking at me already.

She takes a sip of tea.

*You see those two sitting by the window? Aren't they fat? Both of them! I don't know which one's fatter, him or her. Mind you, it's not surprising, is it? I've been watching them ever since I came in, and they've never stopped eating. They've had umpteen courses already and they're still at it. ... I blame the parents. This lot have been over-eating since they were kids – you mark my words! It becomes a habit. And it shows, my goodness! Look at the size of them! Legs like tree-trunks, bulging stomach, bosom like two barrage balloons – and that's only the man! She's as bad. How on earth do they ever get together – well, you know what I mean! When did they last see their feet? And the way she's dressed! No-one that size should dress like that – short skirt with those legs! Anyone would think it's the middle of summer – well, actually it is the middle of summer, but that's no excuse. Not with a figure like that! I don't know! When she looks in the mirror she must see some slim little thing, not the way she is. Some people!

She looks round, then talks confidentially.

That couple over there, just two tables away from me – they haven't said a word to each other since they came in. I would have heard them, being so near. But they haven't, not a word. And they've been here nearly an hour and they're on their coffee. Not a word from either of them. What's up there, I wonder? … Money! That's the answer – I've seen it before. She's spending too much money on clothes and things and he doesn't like it. Doesn't matter which way round, it spells disaster. I wouldn't give them more than six months before they split up. … Oh, they're going now – still not saying a word … .

She looks round again.

That waiter's getting on my nerves.   (*pause*)

Oho, look at those two just coming in! He must be old enough to be her father. Maybe he is her father! No, not from the way she's flashing her eyes at him! No way! Now he must be seventy if he's a day, and she – well, you can't tell with her, maybe thirty, maybe more. He's rich: you can tell – gold rings on his fingers, big cigar – oh, he's rich all right! And she? Well, she's a tart. No other word for it. Dyed blonde, made up so you can't guess what her real face looks like, skirt just about covering her bottom – and up top! – Well, you could get lost in that cleavage! You can see what's going on there. She's on to a good thing, she is. Oh, yes, she knows what she's doing. She makes him feel young, gives him a good time, wears him out, and when he pops off, she comes into all his money. It's an old, old story. … Look at the way she's cuddling up to him – it's unnecessary in public. And the way she looks at him with those boobs! Oh yes, I've got them summed up all right!

Oh, the waiter's looking at me again. He reckons it's time I went and left the table for someone else. Can't blame him really. I have been here an hour and a half over my cup of tea. (*She rises.*) Well, enough watching the world go by for today. … Back to my little world – my bed-sit – just me and my cat.   (*She goes.*)

CURTAIN

* To avoid possible offence with certain audiences, the following paragraph may be substituted (or may alternatively be inserted as an extra).

Look at those two kids racing around all over the place. And the parents sitting there, just smiling at them, if you please. No control, no discipline these days: the kids do what they like. Those parents are piling up trouble for themselves, believe you me! The boy is mischief: you can see it in his eyes. Marks my words, in ten years' time he'll be one of those who pinches cars, takes them for joy-rides and ends up a danger to themselves and other people. And the girl? Heaven knows what she'll get up to when she's a teenager. All that clubbing, or whatever they call it, and getting into trouble. The parents won't be smiling then. Oh no, they certainly won't.

The story of Guinevere

[Began life as a song for 'torch singer' and chorus in a 1976 CPT Revue; converted to a poem for TAP, first performed by the Verse Choir in 1999. Read as a solo in Own Original Poem category in Buckingham Drama Festival, 2002, winning joint First place.]

Long ago when life was tumultuous
Lived a queen who was highly adulterous.
She never felt a twinge of shame,
And Guinevere was the lady's name.

> *Oh, Guinevere! No, Guinevere!*
> *She didn't know and she didn't care.*
> *She never searched for the Holy Grail:*
> *Her interests were wholly male.*

Guinny was King Arthur's spouse:
She shared his realm and she shared his house:
She shared his board but not his bed
And acted like she wasn't wed.

> *Pert Guinevere! Flirt Guinevere!*
> *She sought men far and she sought them near.*
> *Life was good, with all things found,*
> *So she spread her favours all around.*

Now Arthur's court was famous for
The Knights he gathered by the score.
They were the cream of chivalry
And Guinny said 'That lot's for me!'

> *Tut, Guinevere! Slut Guinevere!*
> *She sought men there and she sought them here.*
> *She seduced poetic Galahad,*
> *And changed his style from verse to bad.*

One fine night she wandered nigh
A shady wood that grew nearby
And there in that enchanted spot
She met a knight called Lancelot.

> *Vamp Guinevere! Tramp Guinevere!*
> *She had no scruples and she showed no fear.*
> *The autumn leaves served them for bed:*
> *She lost her heart and she lost her head.*

Now Lancelot he was Arthur's pal:
He should have lain off Arthur's gal.
But he would say, the dirty tyke,
Friends should share and share alike.

Bad Guinevere! Mad Guinevere!
Her design was crystal clear.
When Lancelot drew Excalibur
She said 'Call it what you like': it suited her.

This went on, year out, year in.
They got deeper steeped in sin.
No-one ever found them out
And that is what this tale's about.

So Guinevere? Oh, Guinevere!
She didn't know and she didn't care.
The principle we'd recommend
Is never trust your wife with your best friend.

The other moral you won't miss
Is 'Heaven help a marriage with a wife like this!'.

If Shakespeare were writing today …
(with compliments to the Bard)

[Written in 1999 for TAP Revue. Won Distinction placings in
Solo Verse category at Buckingham Drama Festival 1999, and in
Solo Drama category in Milton Keynes Festival 2000]

To buy – or not to buy?   That is the problem;
Whether to seek some peace of mind and purchase now,
And see that dress hang proudly in my wardrobe,
Or take a chance by waiting for the sales
And hope to find it cheaper.
A risk. For I would not forgive myself
The heartache and the thousand sad regrets
Were I to lose this dress – an outcome far
Too sad to contemplate. To buy? To wait?
To wait – perhaps to lose? Yes, there's the rub!
Would I again encounter such a dress?

Yet – waiting might yield up a wider choice,
The unexpected bargains of a sale,
A fuller range of colours or of style,
A length to match the fashions of the time,
A costume that would dazzle envious eyes,
But earn approval from my dearest friends.

To buy now would leave me safe but sorry.
Decision time! Yes, I must quit the store,
Replace my Barclaycard, close up my purse,
Walk swiftly to the exit, head held high,
Secure in my decision, doubts dispelled …

Yet, at the very door I hesitate,
The vision of that dress before my eyes.
Despite myself, I turn and ask again –
To buy or not to buy … ?

Three monologues: 'Poems for today':

[Written for TAP and performed in second Revue, **TAP into Crime,** October 1998]

1   *Understanding the young*

What is it with the young these days?
Why are they so – apart?
Where did they learn these 'modern' ways?
When did all this start?
Why do they think they're always right?
Why are they all so impolite?
I think it's something to discuss,
Why the young are not like us.

Can't understand the young today.
What do they mean by 'cool'?
Their manners fill me with dismay.
What did they learn at school?
Girls' skirts surely can't get shorter.
They think the Spice girls walk on water.
Won't give their seat up on a bus.
Why on earth aren't they like us?

What is it these days with the young?
They put rings through their noses!
Why do they seem so highly strung?
Why do they strike such poses?
They drink directly from the bottle
And their speech is oh! so glottal.
It's not my place to make a fuss –
But why, oh why, aren't they like us?

I'm worried by the young today.
They're always in a crowd.
Small wonder that they're led astray.
And their music is so loud!
Lads with haircuts like Mohicans,
Girls' hair blazing red like beacons!
It all continues to nonplus –
Why the young are not like us.

2   Waiting for the wife

Waiting for the wife? –
I'm always waiting for the wife!
We've a dinner invitation!
I must curb my irritation;
Keep my blood-pressure steady
While she takes hours getting ready,
And I'm waiting for the wife.

Waiting for the wife –
This is the story of my life!
She meets a friend out walking:
They spend the next hour talking,
And as I watch them nattering
My thoughts are none too flattering,
But – I wait there for the wife.

Waiting for the wife –
It sometimes cuts me like a knife.
When we spend the morning shopping,
Every dress shop mean she's stopping,
And no matter how time presses,
She'll try on twenty dresses –
And I wait there for the wife.

Waiting for the wife.
It could be a cause of strife!
Whether shopping, chatting, preening,
Time for her can lose its meaning.
It can be infuriating,
But I'll no doubt go on waiting,
Always waiting for the wife!

3   If I won the lottery

If I ever won the lottery,
I wonder what I'd do.
Would I carry on as usual?
Or would my life begin anew?
Would it change my personality?
Would I be spoiled by fame?
Would my friends still recognise me?
Or would I stay the same?.

If I came into all that money
What would I use it for?
Would I live a life of luxury?
Would I give it to the poor?
Should I give it all to charity?
Or support some worthy cause?
Get mentioned in the papers
And earn myself applause?

Should I share it with the family,
Pay their mortgages and such?
Should I share it all out equally?
Would they expect too much?
But if I use all the money
For the good of other folk,
I'll end up where I started,
Just like I am now – broke!

It wouldn't be too sensible
To give it all away.
Better to keep part of it
Just for a rainy day.
– And I'll need looking after
 When I'm old and on the shelf!
So now I've thought it over –
I'll keep the lot myself.

Soaps

[Written about 1990 and performed in an OTG Revue; then in 1998 by TAP in their first Revue, **With a Little bit of Luck.**]

I watch Soaps – all the Soaps.
I watch the ones on BBC,
And Channel 4 and ITV.
I never get fed up with them:
I breakfast, lunch and sup with them.
All my dreams and hopes come from Soaps.

I love Soaps – any Soaps.
Life in Coronation Street
Is sometimes bitter, sometimes sweet.
And all those goings-on in Brookside.
(Now there's a Soap on the de-luxe side!)
You need to know the ropes about Soaps.

I need Soaps – hooked on Soaps.
Twice a day I switch on Neighbours;
Share their lives and loves and labours.
Won't miss those stories in East Enders,
Of publicans and market vendors.
Life's kaleidoscopes are in Soaps.

I lived Soaps – super-soaps.
Soaps like Dynasty and Dallas,
With that J.R. just oozing malice!
Sometimes I'd like to be Alexis
And fight the battle of the sexes.
Prime Ministers and Popes, all watch Soaps.

I breathe Soaps – can't miss Soaps.
I am never known to fail
To watch twice-weekly Emmerdale.
And though it's nearly every day,
I never miss Home and Away.
I suffer from the mopes, between Soaps.

I watch Soaps – all the Soaps.
I live through other people's stories:
I bask in their reflected glories.
Real life isn't half so thrilling –
I guess my emptiness needs filling.
Can't think how one copes, without Soaps!

Pregnant Pauses

[Began life as *Lament of the Pregnant Ladies,* written for CPT in 1976,
performed by four (young) ladies with pillows suitably deployed;
repeated in the same form by OTG in 1990; converted to its present
form in 1998, for obvious reasons, for TAP's first Revue, **With a Little
bit of Luck**]

I came fresh and green to the Drama Group
Eager to display my Thespian arts.
I came madly keen to the Drama Group,
Hoping I would land some super parts.
But when they chose a play that I adored,
Including just the role I'd love to play,
Every time my expectations soared
A little something turned up in the way.

I was hoping to play Cleopatra,
A part full of passion and rage.
But with a husband like mine
Who could not draw the line
It was safer to make love on stage.
Why was I so easily led?
So amenable when we're in bed?
I'd have played Cleopatra
If not for that flatterer
But heck! I was pregnant instead.

Two years later I read Desdemona.
She perished through jealousy's curse.
Her husband was jealous,
But mine was too zealous!
I can't decide which is the worse.
I'd surely have bolted the door
If I'd known what was in store.
I'd have played Desdemona
If I'd been a loner
But heck! – I was pregnant once more.

Four years later I tried for Saint Joan,
Whose voices led to her sad fate.
If I'd vowed not to hear
That soft voice in my ear
I wouldn't have got in that state.
Why did it have to be then?
I should have learned to say 'When'!
I'd have acted Saint Joan
If I'd slept on my own,
But heck! – I was pregnant again.

I'd have played all those parts to perfection
And earned my due share of applause.
But with increasing thickness
And mid-morning sickness
My hopes all became a lost cause.

I had three lovely children instead …
Though I'm firmly resolved, come what may,
Since my love for the stage is not dead,
That I'll play Lady Bracknell one day!

Alternative last four lines for older person:

But all that belongs in the past:
My ambition is nearing its peak.
I fulfil my potential at last –
For I play Lady Bracknell next week!

Part 2

Verses for choral speaking

Introduction

The term *Choral speaking* refers to presentation of poetry, song (or even prose pieces) by a group using the speaking voice, rather than the singing voice. The Group may therefore be known as a *Verse Choir* or *Speech Choir*. Certain Drama Festivals include a Choral Speaking category in their repertoire: notably Milton Keynes, Burnley, and Blackburn (where it is known as *Choric Speaking*).

Some Festival Adjudicators make a distinction between pure Choral speaking and dramatic speaking, the difference being the amount of action or gesture included, perhaps analogous to the difference between Oratorio and Opera.

As a performance medium it can be very effective, and great fun to develop. A choir leader must rehearse the Choir, exercising every technique familiar to singing Choirs: pitch, rhythm, pace syncopation, part-speaking, harmonies, and so on. The TAP Choir uses small files or cue-cards with the words and parts marked on, rather like song-sheets. Obviously it can be even more effective if the words and parts are memorized.

The item *Twelve days to Christmas* in the following Section is marked with the original parts allocated to the nine speakers of the TAP Verse Choir of 2002.

Part 2 Verses for choral speaking

First-night blues

[Began as a song in 1982 for CPT, then converted to a poem in 1998 for TAP – not yet performed in this form.]

Why did I want to be an actress?
Why did I ever think that I could act?
Now what started off as merest fantasy
Is shortly turning into grimmest fact.
Will I trip up or miss my opening line?
Will the audience shift their feet or start to laugh?
Will I be the one to cause disaster
Even though I'm only on for a minute and a half …

> *I've got those first-night blues,*
> *Want to run away and hide,*
> *And consider suicide.*
> *Can't cope with all those cues.*
> *I've got those first-night blues.*

> *I've got those first-night nerves,*
> *Got shivers down my spine,*
> *Can't recall my opening line.*
> *I've run out of reserves.*
> *I've got those first-night nerves.*

Half an hour to curtain:
I'm absolutely certain
I'm never going to get through.
I've got an upset tummy,
I think I want my Mummy!
Show me the way to the loo.

> *I've got those first-night shakes,*
> *Next time I'll act my age*
> *And do a job backstage.*
> *I've not got what it takes.*
> *I've got those first-night shakes.*

I'm in a first-night state,
My assets are all stripped,
Where did I put my script?
I've too much on my plate.
I'm in a first-night state.

I'm in a first-night mood,
To think I'm here by choice!
I'm going to lose my voice.
I'm scared of getting booed.
I'm in a first-night mood.

I'm heading for a blackout:
I think I've put my back out.
But who the hell wants to know?
I think I'm going to throw up.
I wish the place would blow up.
That would be the end of the show!

I'm in a first-night daze,
I'm paralyzed with fright,
I can't tell left from right.
I'm seeing through a haze
I'm in a first-night daze.

I'm in a first-night whirl,
My mind is just a blank:
And I've got the show to thank.
I'm anybody's girl … !
I'm in a first-night whirl.

I'm in a first-night sweat,
I'd crawl into a hole.
I'm scared I'll lose control:
I think my pants are wet.
I'm in a first-night sweat.

I've come without my make-up:
I wish that I could wake up
To find it's all a bad dream.
I've got into a panic;
Guess my depression's manic.
Will someone hear if I scream?   (*She screams.*)

30

I've got those first-night blues,
It's not my idea of fun:
And the show's not yet begun!
I'm taking to the booze.
I've got those first-night blues;
Oh yes! Oh, help!
I've got those first-night blues.

Extracts from *Behind the Drama*

[For origin, see Part 4; these five verses selected as a version for TAP Verse Choir to meet timing for the Milton Keynes Drama Festival, January, 1999. The author suggests a further concluding verse: it would be perfectly possible to make a different selection to taste or need.]

Decisions! Decisions!
We need to reach decisions.
Abandon our divisions,
Speak with a single voice.
This is the time to rally;
We dare not shilly-shally.
No time to make revisions.
We have to state a choice.

Conclusion! Conclusion!
We've reached a clear conclusion!
We've cleared up all confusion:
We're truly off the fence,
We've weighed up all the factors
Pray God we find the actors!
We're under no illusion.
Let battle now commence!

Auditions! Auditions!
Oh, how I hate auditions!
These people with ambitions
To venture on the stage.
These would-be Prima donnas
All seeking acting honours:
I have these premonitions
That nothing will assuage!

Rehearsing! Rehearsing!
Oh how I loathe rehearsing!
Our actors need coercing,
They put me in a rage.
That unrewarding slogging!
That endless pettifogging!
Small wonder that I'm cursing,
It adds years to my age!

Beginners! Beginners!
Lights up on Beginners.
You're all illusion-spinners,
Now create that magic spell!
The citadel needs storming!
Yes – the audience are warming!
They're either for us or agin' us!
So go on and give them Hell!

Author's suggested final verse:

Applauding! Applauding!
The audience are applauding!
They've found it all rewarding:
They're singing songs of praise!
We've got them all enraptured!
They're well and truly captured!
They're lavish in their lauding.
It shows that talent pays!

Thirteen Widow Women

[Written in a naughty mood (date uncertain) after reading a history of the town of Reading. The record showed that in addition to brethren and others, the *Hospitium* (a part of Reading Abbey) housed 'thirteen poor widows of the town'. Performed in TAP's third Revue, **Bits and Pieces**, in April, 1999]

Thirteen widow women,
Bereft of worldly wealth,
Rely on holy charity
To keep them in good health.
The monks arrive with offerings
Into which we need not delve …
One only has to beckon –
And then there are twelve.

Twelve widow women
Await with bated breath
The summons to communion:
It's a better fate than death.
One monk claims to offer
A shorter cut to Heaven …
He merely lifts an eyebrow –
And that makes eleven.

Eleven widow women
Are anxious to impress,
For every monthly visit
Gives them something to confess.
The monks on holy business
Are just like other men …
One only lifts his cassock –
And then there are ten.

Ten widow women
So prematurely chaste:
The monks sing lamentations,
Think it really is a waste.
One widow is a stunner,
Her proportions are divine …
They go to fetch the Abbot –
And then there are nine.

Nine widow women
To soothe those holy brows,
And nine remaining prelates
Forget their solemn vows.
Four weeks of self-denial
Have left them in a state …
One begs for absolution –
And that makes it eight.

Eight widow women
With nothing much to lose,
Seek benefit of clergy,
Have eight from which to choose.
Eight expectant fathers
To near-despair are driven …
One sheds his holy habit –
And then there are seven.

Seven widow women
Await the call to arms,
And seven excited clerics
Are eager for their charms.
They want to be lay-brethren
And get up to monkish tricks …
One only has to whistle –
And then there are six.

Six widow women
Expect a monk's embrace,
But the other monks are novices
Who fear the fall from grace.
The widows tire of waiting,
Ask 'How IS salvation won?'
Decide 'Let's go and get it!'
And so there are none.

Twelve days to Christmas

[Written for the 6th TAP Revue in December 2002. The markings refer to the Voices used by the Verse Choir: initials of individuals; Back Row; Front Row; and so on.]

All (There are twelve days to Christmas,
(Still a great deal to be done.
T (I've got a list a mile long
(And I've hardly yet begun.
    Bk No cause yet to worry
    Fr No need yet to hurry.
All Christmas preparations are always lots of fun.

All (Now it's ten days to Christmas,
D (Time I started on mince pies.
(But I'm short of key ingredients,
(Though of course that's no surprise.
    All (See this needs careful planning.
    (The barricades need manning!
D I've got to do more shopping for the missing merchandise.

All (There are eight days to Christmas.
(Now how many will we be?
S (Must not forget to order us
(A good-sized Christmas tree.
    Bk Wherever should we place it?
    Fr However do we space it?
All Will there be room enough by the settee?

All (There are six days to Christmas
(And time is running short.
Bet (I've not got the Christmas pudding yet
(And more things I should have bought.
    (The to-ing and the fro-ing!
    (The puffing and the blowing!
Bet (I have a feeling things are getting fraught.

All (It's only four days to Christmas
(And still nothing's going right.
C (Still a few more days to go, though.
(Can't give up without a fight.
    (I'm getting close to panic.
    (I'm nearly going manic.
C (No wonder I can't get to sleep at night.

All There are just two days to Christmas
A (And I'm going round the bend.
(I've organised things badly
(No, it's useless to pretend.
(The bloody lights keep fusing.
(And my husband sits there snoozing
A (I can only pray we'll get there in the end.

All (There are no days to Christmas
(Because Christmas morning's here!
D (It seems my prayers were answered
(And we're full of Christmas cheer!

D	The oven is heated,
C	The company's seated,
S	The presents await us.
Bet	Decorations elate us,
S	The turkey is browning,
A	My husband's stopped frowning,
S	The kids are behaving,
T	The banners are waving.
All	The drinks are before us.

(enter rest of Company offering trays of drinks)
Men So – pray silence for the chorus!

(all cast raise drinks and sip toast)
All Merry Christmas and a very good New Year!

A plea to the Queen

[This poem was written in September 1999 especially for the U3A Christmas party close to the Millennium. City status went to Wolverhampton and others. To date Milton Keynes is still hoping to re-apply. While not suitable for further performance, this piece is included for historical and amusement value.]

Your Majesty, please hear our story.
We're hoping for a touch of glory.
Grant us, please, what should await us:
Give Milton Keynes its City Status.

Say the word that will elate us:
Milton Keynes for City status!

Milton Keynes, we know, is booming;
Its employment figures zooming;
Progress-wise we're sitting pretty.
Shouldn't we then be a city?

Please heed the call within this ditty:
Make Milton Keynes the next new City!

Milton Keynes just goes on growing.
There's no evidence of slowing.
No-one dares to underrate us –
We are ripe for City status.

Say the word that will elate us:
Milton Keynes for City status!

We can challenge any rival:
We can guarantee survival.
We've lots of money in the kitty.
We deserve to be a City.

Please heed the call within this ditty:
Make Milton Keynes the next new City!

Everyone knows where you can find us.
Ipswich, Luton, lag behind us.
Other towns will no doubt hate us
If we win our City status.

> *Say the word that will elate us:*
> *Milton Keynes for City status!*

We pray our plea won't go unheeded
Your approval's just what's needed.
Let's get down to the nitty-gritty –
Milton Keynes *should* be a City!

> *Please heed the call within this ditty:*
> *Make Milton Keynes the next new City!*

Your Majesty, look kindly on us:
Let this honour land upon us.
Let the country celebrate us
When you grant us City status.

> *Say the word that will elate us:*
> *Milton Keynes for City status!*

We're a credit to our planners:
We are proud to raise our banners
To miss this chance would be a pity
Why not make us the Millennium City?

Don't put your Grandma on the stage

[In Summer 2000, TAP were busy reviewing 20th century drama, in order to contribute to the MK U3A Exhibition **All our Yesterdays**. Inspired by the words of Noël Coward, Pip could not resist writing his own version for the TAP Verse Choir, thinking ahead to the U3A Christmas party that same year!]

Don't put your Grandma on the stage, Mrs Worthington,
Don't put your Granny on the stage.
She's terribly keen to be in a play,
But really it's rather late in the day.
To give the dear old girl her due,
She's pretty good for ninety-two.
But please explain with utmost tact,
She's getting far too old to act.
Forget the past: it's time to turn the page –
So please don't put your Grandma on the stage.

Don't put your Grandma on the stage, Mrs Worthington,
Don't put your Granny on the stage.
Her hearing aid is on the blink,
And she's getting a bit too fond of drink,
So that her diction, once admired,
Now leaves a lot to be desired.
Accept the ravages of time:
She's more than a little bit past her prime.
She'd send the poor Director in a rage –
So please don't put your Grandma on the stage.

Don't put your Grandma on the stage, Mrs Worthington,
Don't put your Granny on the stage.
I fear her assets are all stripped.
She's more than likely to lose her script.
And she is just a little bit lame –
That is, without her zimmer-frame.
She's most unlikely to learn her lines,
So before the rest of the cast resigns,
Persuade her to come to terms with her age.
Just don't put your Grandma on the stage, Mrs Worthington,
Don't put your Granny on the stage.

Part 3
Sketches and duologues

Part 3   Sketches and duologues

On Midsummer Boulevard

[One of several *Scenes of Milton Keynes* life penned around 1990, just for fun, this scene was in the first TAP show, **With a Little bit of Luck**, in 1997 and repeated at different venues in 1998 and 1999, with a cast change. It could be applied to any new shopping precinct with very minor changes to title and script.]

Characters

Mrs E   **Mrs H**

Mrs H, carrying two heavy shopping bags, and Mrs E, carrying one small one, meet.

Mrs E   Hullo, Mrs H! Long time no see. Been shopping?

Mrs H (*indicating her load*) What do you think this is? Weight-lifting?

Mrs E (*oblivious to sarcasm*) I've been shopping as well.

Mrs H   We always shop on Friday, Jim and me.

Mrs E   Fancy your husband going shopping with you!

Mrs H   We don't mind the shopping centre because he can sit down outside and wait for me. He never went shopping with me when we lived in Manchester. I mean, where could he sit down in the middle of Piccadilly?

Mrs E   Where is he, then, your Jim?

Mrs H   Forgot his fags. Left me carrying this lot while he nipped back – typical!

Mrs E   I never take my Bert shopping with me – not any more!

Mrs H   Why ever not?

Mrs E   Not in the big stores. I'm afraid of him getting lost.

Mrs H   Getting lost?

Mrs E	He does! Wanders up and down between the counters, looking all lost and pathetic.
Mrs H	You could ask him to meet you at the checkout, or outside, like my Jim does.
Mrs E	Well … he forgets what I look like.
Mrs H	Forgets what you look like?
Mrs E	That's what he says.
Mrs H	… and you believe him?
Mrs E	Oh yes! More than once, when I used to take him shopping, I'd see him following some woman out into the street and it wouldn't be me at all.
Mrs H	Well, I can understand that …
Mrs E	So I don't take him no more.
Mrs H	(*looking around*) Where is that husband of mine? … I expect you see enough of your Bert in the evenings. My Jim don't spend an evening at home these days. He's always up in the Leisure Centre, playing snooker. Every evening till half-past ten. – No, I tell a lie! Fridays and Saturdays he's at the pub, playing darts. – I tell you, Mrs E., I hardly ever see him in the evenings. – O-ooh, it's such a relief!
Mrs E	Now you mention it, I haven't seen much of Bert lately.
Mrs H	Why, what does he do?
Mrs E	Bert? He's up the loft.
Mrs H	What!
Mrs E	Up in the loft.
Mrs H	Oh, I thought you said 'up aloft'. Gave me a shock for a minute. Thought you meant he'd passed on.
Mrs E	Oh, no. I would have told you.
Mrs H	Here! Wait a minute! You haven't got a loft!
Mrs E	Yes, we have.
Mrs H	You've got one of them flat roofs.
Mrs E	We did have, 'till a month ago. That's when they put a proper roof on.

Mrs H (*ironically*) On account of the indoor rainfall!

Mrs E   That's right! So we've got a loft now. Bert wouldn't be up in the loft if we hadn't got one.

Mrs H   You must have been in a right old mess for a while, then.

Mrs E   Oh, yes, we were. We had workmen in the house for weeks.

Mrs H   That was nice for you.

Mrs E   It was! We used to have lovely chats over a cup of tea. One of the men was ever so handsome. … used to work with his shirt off, he did … all sunburn and muscles … (*dreamily*) he was gorgeous! … One afternoon, Bert wasn't home yet and there was just this workman and me. I looked at him – and he looked at me – and I could see that look in his eyes …

Mrs H (*intrigued*) Well, what happened?

Mrs E   I ran! I didn't half run … I've never run so fast in my life … but I couldn't catch up with him.

Mrs H   Well, well! Still waters … ! (*looking around*) Come on, Jim, it don't take that long to pick up a packet of fags. … What's your Bert doing up in the loft, then?

Mrs E   I don't really know.

Mrs H   Maybe he just wants to get away from you for a bit.

Mrs E   It's some kind of do-it-yourself, I think. Anyway, he loves going up the loft … like this afternoon, soon after The Archers finished – you know, the repeat – he went up then. I left him up there.

Mrs H   As long as he's doing something useful!

Mrs E (*suddenly, after a pause*) Wait a minute! It wasn't this afternoon that Bert went up the loft. It was yesterday evening.

Mrs H (*staring at her in disbelief*) Yesterday evening! – And you've not seen him since?

Mrs E   No.

Mrs H   Not exactly under your feet all the time, is he? More like above your head.

Mrs E (*thinking it out*) That's right. It must have been yesterday evening, because it was the first time I heard that bit about Eddie Grundy, not the second time. I remember now. … O-ooh, I do love listening to *The Archers.*

Mrs H   Never mind *The Archers*! What about your Bert?

Mrs E   He's been up there all that time.

Mrs H   I can't believe that. What was to stop him getting down?

Mrs E   No … well, except I've just remembered …

Mrs H   What?

Mrs E   I took the ladder away.

Mrs H   You … ? What on earth for?

Mrs E   To get to the top shelf in the kitchen. There was a box of chocolate brazil nuts up there and I just fancied them. I do love chocolate brazil nuts, don't you?

Mrs H   Never mind chocolate brazil nuts! Bert can yell, can't he?

Mrs E   Yes, but I wouldn't hear him this far away, would I?

Mrs H (*getting exasperated*) But when you're home … ?

Mrs E   I'd never hear him with the telly on.

Mrs H   Well, hadn't you better get home a bit double-quick? He might be getting a bit desperate by now.

Mrs E   Yes, perhaps I'd better.

Mr H   I should think so, too! Anyway, I can see my Jim coming at last. Go on! Off you go!

Mrs E   Yes. Bye-bye, Mrs H. Nice talking to you. Maybe see you next week.   (*Mrs H goes off R.*)

… Oh dear, I've forgotten to get my lottery ticket. I'd better get it now.

She follows Mrs H off.

CURTAIN

A Question of Dress

[This duologue formed part of TAP's second Revue, **TAP into Crime**, in October 1998.]

Characters

Mrs A	**Mrs B**

Mrs A   Oh! Hello, we meet again!

Mrs B   Enjoyed ourselves last night, didn't we?

Mrs A   We always do.

Mrs B   True!

Mrs A   Nice today, isn't it?

Mrs B   Certainly better than yesterday.

Mrs A begins to stare fixedly at Mrs B's dress: Mrs B looks uncertain.

Am I showing something I shouldn't?

Mrs A   No, it isn't that.

She slowly circles Mrs B.

Mrs B   Well, what are you sniffing round me like that for?

Mrs A   I – I don't like to say.

Mrs B   Something's bothering you.

Mrs A tries to peer inside the neck of the dress.

Here! What are you doing?

Mrs A lifts up the hem of the skirt. Mrs B reacts strongly.

Stop it! Anyone would think you was one of those!

Mrs A   One of what?

Mrs B   No, of course not: you've been married for years!

Mrs A   What are you talking about?

Mrs B   Oh, never mind! Now come on, what is it?

Mrs A   I find it very embarrassing!

Mrs B   You find it embarrassing! What about me?

Mrs A   That's my dress!

Mrs B   Eh?

Mrs A (*embarrassed*) You're wearing my dress.

Mrs B   What did you say?

Mrs A   What are you doing in my dress?

Mrs B   Your dress?

Mrs A   That's the dress I bought to go on holiday three years ago.

Mrs B   Three years! If I'd known it was that old I wouldn't have touched it.

Mrs A   How could you?

Mrs B   What do you mean – how could I?

Mrs A   I wouldn't have thought it of you, not after all our years of friendship!

Mrs B   What are you on about? There was plenty to choose from. I might have had any dress.

Mrs A   Oh! … Shameless! Coming into my house; rummaging around in my wardrobe when I'm not looking; and making off with one of my dresses, without even a by-your-leave!

Mrs B   I did what? You want to watch your words, friendship or no friendship. Making accusations like that! There's a law of libel, you know!

Mrs A   You mean you didn't take it from my house?

Mrs B   Of course not! When was I last in your house?

Mrs A   Well, how did you get it then?

Mrs B   You might have guessed – (*a little reluctantly*) I bought it at the Oxfam shop.

Mrs A   The Oxfam shop? But I never took it to the Oxfam shop. How did they get hold of it? Who's been taking my dresses to the Oxfam shop?

Mrs A   Look, how do you know it is your dress? They don't make only one of each kind, you know. Look, when you get home, have a good look in your wardrobe. It's probably fallen down the back somewhere.

Mrs A I know because there's some stitching gone just inside the neck and a dirty mark on the hem that I couldn't get out.

Mrs A (*indignantly*) Oh, if I'd noticed that I certainly would never have bought it. It was on the good-as-new rail and all.

Mrs A (*after a pause*) It was Jim!

Mrs B Your husband?

Mrs A Yes. It's beginning to make sense. It was Jim who took it.

Mrs B But why?

Mrs A I remember saying about the mark on the hem and how if it was cleaned it would be as good as new.

Mrs B You're not saying that he thought you meant it to go on the good-as-new rail at the Oxfam shop?

Mrs A (*eyes narrowing*) He may say that, that he misunderstood me, but I know my Jim better. He never liked that dress – said it showed too much! He did this deliberately.

Mrs B You want to keep your husband under better control, you do!

Mrs A (*not liking this*) Yes. Well … just wait till I see him!

Mrs B That's that, then. I wouldn't be seen dead in it now.

Mrs A I can have it back, then?

Mrs B You can – for what I paid for it.

Mrs A You expect me to pay for my own dress?

Mrs B Well, I had to pay for it, didn't I?

Mrs A You didn't have to buy it.

Mrs B It was for sale, for heaven's sake! And I didn't know it was your dress. And just remember, if I hadn't bought it and some one else had, you'd never have had the chance of getting it back. You ought to thank me.

Mrs A Oh – there's something in that.

Mrs B Three pounds, please.

Mrs A I see – (*thoughtful*) does your Phil know you buy dresses second-hand at charity shops?

Mrs B (*uncomfortable*) Well, no, I don't tell him everything.

Mrs A (*on the offensive*) I know your Phil. We were discussing all these charity shops at the pub one evening, I remember. 'My wife doesn't need to go to charity shops', he said. He's very proud like that, isn't he?

Mrs B (*uneasy*) Yes, he is, a bit. He'd go mad, actually, if he knew.

Mrs A You want to keep your husband under better control, you do!

Mrs B Point taken!

Mrs A Tell you what – you keep the dress.

Mrs B But I don't want the dress now – especially now I know it's yours.

Mrs A Yes, that's it. You keep the dress. But when I see you both at the pub tonight, I'll say, 'Phil, how do you like your wife's new dress that she bought at the Oxfam shop?'

Mrs B You wouldn't!

Mrs A I would!

Mrs B (*after a pause*) Oh, all right, you can have the dress back for two pounds, but not a word to Phil, mind!

Mrs A One pound!

Mrs B (*after a pause*) Look, for friendship's sake, I'll get the dress back to you and we'll forget the money. Tell you what – you can buy a double round at the pub tonight.

Mrs A Done!

They shake hands on it and walk off together.

(*as they go*) Husbands!

Mrs B Husbands!

CURTAIN

Evening Surgery

[Written for and performed in the U3A Show, **Jubilations**, May, 2002.]

Characters

The Doctor   **Mrs Williams**
                        (the patient, gloomy, cockney)

The scene is a Doctor's surgery. The Doctor is seated. (S)he consults a list, rises and goes to the door.

Doctor Mrs Williams, please!   (*Mrs Williams enters.*)

Good afternoon, Mrs Williams. Do sit down.   (*Both sit.*)

Now, what's the trouble?

Mrs W (*gloomily*) Depression.

Doctor Oh! Why do you think you're depressed?

Mrs W It's diarrhoea.

Doctor Well, we can do something about that. Is it something you've eaten?

Mrs W Eh?

Doctor (*starting to make out a prescription*) … that's given you diarrhoea.

Mrs W Nothin' like that. I said it's dire 'ere. Mind you, it's dire everywhere. It's just that things are getting' on top o' me.

Doctor Why is that, do you think?

Mrs W I got worries.

Doctor Well, I can hardly prescribe for your worries

Mrs W It's 'ernia.

Doctor Oh, that's different.

Mrs W It's my mother-in-law.

Doctor (*taken aback*) Your mother-in-law's the one with a hernia?

Mrs W She lives with us, you see.

Doctor   No. I don't see …

Mrs W   She gets on my nerves. I just can't stand 'er near.

Doctor (*intrigued*) Yes – well – very awkward for your husband.

Mrs W   'E's in the middle, isn' 'e?

Doctor   Yes, of course.

Mrs W   We 'ad a terrible row the other day, 'er and me. 'E 'eard it all.

Doctor   Bound to affect him.

Mrs W   Sentimental!

Doctor   He must have feelings for his mother.

Mrs W   'E went mad! That's what I said – it sent 'im mental! Smashed two plates and a saucer, 'e did.

Doctor   I don't see how I can …

Mrs W   Took 'im a week to calm down.

Doctor   Well, that's something you'll have to sort out between you.

Mrs W   That's just it. Wertigo.

Doctor (*puzzled*) You have trouble with heights?

Mrs W   Heights? No.

Doctor   I thought you mentioned vertigo?

Mrs W   No. It's my problem – where to go? Where to go from 'ere.

Doctor   How do you react to your husband's bad temper, Mrs Williams?

Mrs W   Ice-cream.

Doctor   You find eating ice-cream calms you down?

Mrs W   No – I scream. I scream my 'ed orf.

Doctor (*making out another prescription*) I can give you something to relax you.

Mrs W   'E's got 'is problems.

Doctor   Your husband?

Mrs W   Yes. 'E's got 'is ecstasy.

Doctor (*sharply*) What! That is not the answer.

Mrs W   Eh?

Doctor   Taking dangerous drugs is not the answer to anything.

Mrs W (*indignant*) My 'usband don't take drugs!

Doctor   I thought you said …

Mrs W   I said 'e's got 'is ex to see! 'Is ex-wife.

Doctor   Oh …

Mrs W   She says 'e still owes 'er money, the bitch.

Doctor   I'm afraid I …

Mrs W   'E's not comfortable.

Doctor   I can understand that.

Mrs W   It's 'is genes, you see.

Doctor   Well, we can't do anything about those.

Mrs W   'Ow do you mean?

Doctor   Well, we're born with those, aren't we?

Mrs W   Oh, no. 'E only bought them last week.

Doctor (*as understanding dawns*) Oh, those jeans!

Mrs W   Yes, too tight around the … you know!

Doctor   Well, that's not a medical matter.

Mrs W   'E's got a lot on 'is mind, my 'usband.

Doctor (*getting weary*) Who hasn't?

Mrs W   'E's got convictions, 'e 'as.

Doctor   Well, it's good to have convictions, but …

Mrs W   'E's only got two.

Doctor   Two convictions?

Mrs W   Both for grievous bodily 'arm. It's 'is temper, you see!

Doctor   Right! – Well, now, Mrs Williams …

Mrs W   One thing made 'im 'appy, though.

Doctor   Really, what was that?

Mrs W (*with some satisfaction*) Geriatric!

Doctor   Your husband's a geriatric?

Mrs W   Not 'im – my son!

Doctor (*lost*) Your son's a geriatric?

Mrs W   My son, Gerry – at football last Sunday. 'E scored a 'at trick

Doctor   Well, well, Mrs Williams, I do have other patients …

Mrs W   … and there's another thing that gets on my nerves.

Doctor (*resigned*) What's that?

Mrs W   Sycophants.

Doctor (*surprised*) Sycophants?

Mrs W   Can't stand 'em. All over the place, they are.

Doctor   What are?

Mrs W   I don't know 'ow they get in.

Doctor (*lost again*) Get in?

Mrs W   Ants! I'm sick of 'em!

Doctor (*completing prescriptions*) Never mind, Mrs Williams, things can only get better.

Mrs W   Don' think so (*suddenly tearful*) Armageddon …

Doctor   Surely not as bad as that?

Mrs W   I'm a geddin' fed up with it all

Doctor (*rising*) That's it, Mrs Williams. Here's your prescription. I've given you something for your diarrhoea; I'm referring you to the hospital for your hernia; there's an inhalant for your vertigo, a relaxant for your screaming fits and a tonic for your depression. But you'll have to go to the hardware store next door for your ant powder.

Doctor ushers her to the door.

Goodbye, Mrs Williams

When she has gone, the Doctor returns to his/her seat, collapses into it, takes a couple of pills in some water, then consults a list and returns to the door.

Mr Jackson, please.

CURTAIN

On the Prom

[Written in 1984, not yet performed]

Characters

Charlie   Billy

The scene is a seaside promenade. Raucous singing is heard off. It is vaguely like I do like to be beside the seaside. *Charlie and Billy stagger on: they are very drunk and swigging from beer-cans.*

Charlie All together now …

Both Oh, we do like to be beside the seaside! We do like to be beside the sea!

Billy (*to someone off*) Hey, Grandma! Do you like to be beside the sisede? Eh? Eh?

Charlie Is he giving you a good time, your old man? Is he? Is he? Eh?

Billy Ignored us, she did, didn't she, Charlie?

Charlie Everybody's ignoring us, aren't they, Billy?

Billy Can't understand why, Charlie. Why isn't everyone happy like us?

Charlie Why aren't they all fell of fullow feeling?

Billy Eh?

Charlie (*re-thinking*) … full of fellow-feeling! Ha-ha! You try saying that quickly, Billy.

Billy The reason why they're not happy like us, Charlie, is because they're sober.

Charlie And we're drunk!

Billy Actually, I'm ashamed of you, Charlie.

Charlie Why're you ashamed of me, Billy?

Billy Because you were going to give up the booze, you were.

Charlie Who said?

Billy You said.

Charlie I said?

Billy   It was one of your New Year Revolutions – that you would give up the booze.

Charlie   When did I say that, Billy?

Billy   At that New Year's Eve party – you remember! On January the second.

Charlie   That explains it, Billy. I'd been drunk for three days. So I wasn't responsible for what I said. Doesn't count! Here's to drink!

They swig away at their beer-cans.

Both (*singing*) Oh I do like to be beside the sea …

Charlie (*leaning over the prom rail*) Hello, darling! Here, Billy, there's a smashing view from up here.

Billy   Now behave yourself, Charlie!

Charlie (*calling*) D'you want some help rubbing in your sun-tan oil, darling? – Oh! Didn't notice you, mate.

They move away a little.

Billy   You shouldn't say things like that, Charlie.

Charlie   Well, I didn't think he was that big.

Billy   Respect for women, Charlie!

Charlie   To the women!

Billy   My wife's a woman.

Charlie   So's mine, Billy. I mean, she always has been. I miss her, Billy.

Billy   No, you don't,. Charlie.

Charlie   I really do, Billy, I really wish my Millie was here.

Billy   But you don't, Charlie. Your Millie thinks you're in Birmingham on a conference.

Charlie (*after a pause*) You're right, Billy! – Do you know what I feel like doing, Billy?

Billy   No, Charlie.

Charlie   Shall I tell you, Billy?

Billy   What, Charlie?

Charlie   … what I feel like doing.

Billy   You can tell me anything, Charlie. I'm your friend.

Charlie   So you are, Billy. You've been my friend for a long time.

Billy   I know that, Charlie.

Charlie   You've been my friend nearly as long as I've been your friend. That's wonderful, Billy!   (*They embrace.*)

Billy   What did you want to tell me, Charlie?

Charlie (*after a pause*) I've forgotten.

Billy   To friendship!

Charlie   I remember what I feel like doing.

Billy   What, Charlie?

Charlie   I feel like having a swim in the sea.

Billy   You haven't got a costume, Charlie.

Charlie   I don't need a costume. I really feel like a swim in the sea.

Billy   It's getting late, Charlie.

Charlie   I'm going to dive off the edge of the prom into the water: that's what I'm going to do.

Billy   I wouldn't, Charlie.

Charlie   I've made up my mind, Billy. I'm going to take off my clothes, and I'm going to dive into the sea. And then I'm going to dive out again.

He begins to strip.

Billy   I don't think you should, Charlie.

Charlie   You don't think I'm capable of diving off the prom into the sea, Billy?

Billy   It isn't that, Charlie …

Charlie   Billy, I was a champion diver when I was at school. I was the best. Don't you remember?

Billy   All the same, Charlie …

Charlie (*earnestly*) You do believe me, that I was the champion diver at school, Billy?

Billy I do believe you, Charlie …

Charlie (*hurt*) How could you forget that I was the champion diver at school, eh, Billy?

Billy I haven't forgotten, Charlie …

Charlie I'm very disappointed in you, Billy. I thought you were my friend.

Billy I am your friend, Charlie – and that's why I tell you you can't dive off the prom into the sea.

Charlie Why not, Billy?

Billy Because the tide's out.

Charlie (*peering*) You're right, Billy. There was plenty of water this morning. Where is it?

Billy It's gone, Charlie.

Charlie Don't blame it! Who would stay in this dump longer than he could help? Come on, Billy, let's go.

Billy Er – Charlie …

Charlie Yes, Billy?

Billy Put your clothes on, Charlie.

Charlie Oh, yes …

> *He dresses, not very successfully, putting his left leg into his right trouser-leg and leaving the other trouser-leg dangling.*

Billy Where shall we go, Charlie?

Charlie I know! There's a disco at that place about five miles up the main road. Let's go there, Charlie.

Billy All right. Too far to walk, though. We'll have to go by car.

Charlie Here's one for the road!   (*They finish off their cans.*)

Billy No point in taking two cars. We'll go in mine.

Charlie No, no, no! Won't hear of it, Billy. We'll go in mine: it's just round the corner.

Billy So's mine. Let's go in mine.

Charlie Tell you what, Billy …

Billy   What, Charlie?

Charlie   We'll compromise, Billy.

Billy   How's that, Charlie?

Charlie   Simple! We'll both go there in my car, and we'll come back in yours!

Billy   Good idea!

They stagger off, singing 'I do like to be beside the seaside, beside the sea … '

CURTAIN OR BLACKOUT

Part 4
Playlets and One-acts

Part 4   Playlets and One-acts

Behind the Drama

[This was presented in full in TAP's first Revue, **With a little bit of Luck**, in April 1998 and later abbreviated by Jocelyn Lord into a purely choral item (see Part 2).]

Characters

The Narrator	**The CAST** (an indeterminate number of **actors**)
The Director	

Throughout the play the Narrator steps forward to deliver the commentaries and retires during the ensuing scene. Cast and Director divide the verses and mime as appropriate.

As the play opens, the Cast are seated in a semicircle. They are arguing vehemently. The Director is among them.

When the Narrator speaks, the noise ceases, but the argument evidently goes on.

Narrator Ladies and gentlemen, observe this group of people.
Who are they, and what are they doing?
Is it the local Chamber of Commerce in earnest conference?No.
Is it a philosophical debate on the Meaning of Life?   No.

Let me enlighten you. It is a meeting of an amateur theatre group, and they are discussing their future – if any!

Look upon them with understanding and sympathy, for what you are witnessing from your behind-the-scenes viewpoint is the prologue to the drama behind the drama:
the tension, the agony, the heart-ache, that are part and parcel of amateur theatricals.

They are choosing their next play ... .   **DECISIONS!**

Cast (*variously*)

Decisions! Decisions!
We need to reach decisions.
Abandon our divisions,
Speak with a single voice.
This is the time to rally;
We dare not shilly-shally.
No time to make revisions.
We have to state a choice.

Selection! Selection!
The problem is selection!
A process of inspection
To find a likely play.
What is it we are after?
Do we go for tears or laughter?
Which is the right direction?
We must decide today.

Conclusion! Conclusion!
We've reached a clear conclusion!
We've cleared up all confusion.
We're truly off the fence,
We've weighed up all the factors.
Pray God we find the actors!
We're under no illusion.
Let battle now commence!

The Cast remove chairs and gather at one side of the stage, leaving only the Director.

Narrator So! The play has been selected – but will they find the actors?
Now follows Act 1 of the drama behind the drama.
It is short, but crucial. It will generate mixed emotions:
at the beginning, from over-confidence to sheer terror:
at the end, from quiet triumph to sullen resentment.

This Act is entitled …   **AUDITIONS.**

The Director takes centre stage. While speaking his three (two?) verses, he takes a chair. [An alternative middle verse may be spoken by a female member of the cast.] Towards the end, the first contender joins him.

Auditions! Auditions!
Oh, how I hate auditions!
These people with ambitions
To venture on the stage.
These would-be *Prima donnas*
All seeking acting honours:
I have these premonitions
That nothing will assuage!

Auditions! Auditions!
Oh, must we have auditions!
I can't help my suspicions
It's all a waste of time.
Why are they so eager?
Their talents are so meagre,
I resent these impositions
It's nothing short of crime!

Auditions! Auditions!
Oh, how I dread auditions!
Be still, my intuitions!
I pray that I can cope.
I guess I must surrender:
Send in the first contender.
It's one of our traditions –
And while there's life, there's hope!

[Alternative second verse for female character]

Auditions! Auditions!
I'm hopeless at auditions!
I lose at competitions.
I know it in advance.
Oh, why was I so eager?
My talents are so meagre.
I've too many inhibitions,
I'll never stand a chance.

During the Narrator's next next speech, the cast are seen one by one by the Director and gather at the other side of the stage.

Narrator   Act Two is the longest and most difficult of all: it is never-ending: it is all-embracing.
It excludes everything else: the day's work is neglected: family life suffers: divorce is threatened.
Patience is tried: endurance is tested: tempers are frayed.

But this is an essential and inescapable part of the drama.
It is called ...   **REHEARSING**.

The Director speaks the first and third verses. The second is shared among the cast.

Rehearsing! Rehearsing!
Oh how I loathe rehearsing!
Our actors need coercing,
They put me in a rage.
That unrewarding slogging!
That endless pettifogging!
Small wonder that I'm cursing,
It adds years to my age!

Rehearsing! Rehearsing!
We don't enjoy rehearsing!
We'd rather be dispersing
And heading for the bar.
Our Director's past enduring,
His temper's beyond curing.
The insults he's disbursing!
Who does he think we are?

Rehearsing! Rehearsing!
Oh, is there *more* rehearsing!
I feel in need of nursing,
My hair is turning grey!
Why are we barrel-scraping?
Now don't just stand there gaping!
And stop all that conversing!
Let's get on with the play!

While the Narrator is speaking, the cast display tension in various ways.

Narrator Rehearsals are finally over: the last act is looming.
The moment of truth is here: there is no turning back.
There is no escape: this is the First Night.
The auditorium is filling: the backstage crew is poised.
The cast is assembled, heart in mouth, praying for a miracle, straining at the leash.

Any moment now, the call will come –   **BEGINNERS, PLEASE!**

The first verse is shared by the cast, the remaining two are for the Director.

Beginners! Beginners!
Any minute it's Beginners.
Have mercy on us sinners!
The show's about to start!
The adrenalin is rising!
Our panic needs disguising!
Call up the strength within us!
Let each one do their part.

Beginners! Beginners!
They're calling for Beginners.
Now go out there as winners!
Here comes your chance to shine.
Just show them what you're made of:
There's nothing you're afraid of!
We've had weeks to discipline us –
Don't forget your opening line!

Beginners! Beginners!
Lights up on Beginners.
You're all illusion-spinners,
Now create that magic spell!
The citadel needs storming!
Yes – the audience are warming!
They're either for us or agin' us!
So go on and give them Hell!

As the Narrator speaks, the cast move on and off, as in performance. By the end, they are gathered together, expectantly.

Narrator And so the play proceeds, smoothly – to everyone's astonishment and delight.
There are no disasters: No-one misses an entrance.
No-one fluffs a line: the scenery does not collapse.
The audience is quiet. Are they attentive, or merely asleep?
Are they appreciative, or merely polite? Has the miracle occurred?
No-one can tell until the final curtain. Will there be …

The last actors return. After a silent moment, loud applause is heard. The final verses are shared.

Applauding! Applauding!
The audience are applauding!
They've found it all rewarding:
They're singing songs of praise!
We've got them all enraptured!
They're well and truly captured!
They're lavish in their lauding.
It shows that talent pays!

We've earned their approbation:
We thrive on approbation!
We hear their acclamation –
Just hark at that applause!
They're putting out the banners!
They're ringing out hosannas!
We bask in admiration!.
We've taken twelve encores!

Listen to that clapping!
We love to hear them clapping,
And get those feet a-tapping.
We've set the place alight!
We have their full approval:
No call for our removal.
Enjoy all that back-slapping!
It's all right on the night!

But when the self-congratulation is over, the Narrator has the last word:

Narrator   But what will it be like on the second night?

CURTAIN OR BLACKOUT

The Rehearsal

[Derived from earlier ideas, this piece was first presented in this form at TAP's first Revue, **With a little bit of luck** , in 1997.]

Characters

J.D. (Director, long-suffering and bad-tempered)

Chris (Stage Manager, excessively cheerful)

Cynthia (Actress, vague)

Kay (Actress, unsure of herself)

Mildred (Actress, apologetic)

The scene is a stage, bare except for chairs. Two are occupied by Kay and Mildred, hunched over their scripts. J.D. is pacing about.

J.D.   Twenty past eight! Where the hell are they? Anyone would think the first night was next month, not next week.

Kay   Cynthia's the one who's usually late. Robert's very punctual.

Chris (*entering*) J.D.!

J.D.   Yes, Chris, what is it?

Chris   Phone message from Robert. He can't make it: he's got the 'flu.

J.D. (*yelling*) You should have told him to turn up, 'flu or no 'flu!

Chris (*cheerfully*) No point shouting at me. I'm only the stage manager.(*exit*)

Mildred   We don't want all of us to catch the 'flu, do we?

J.D. (*exasperated*) We don't want to cancel the bloody play, either!

Mildred   Sorry ...

   Cynthia enters

J.D. (*rounding on her*) Where have you been?

Cynthia   When do you mean? I went to Marks and Spencers this afternoon, but just now I ...

J.D.   It's half-past eight!

Cynthia   Yes, I know, dear. I'm always here punctually at half-past eight.

J.D.   You should be here before half-past eight.

Cynthia   I thought we started at half-past eight.

J.D.   We do! That's very true – we do! But that's because you're never here until half-past eight and we can't start without you. But we're all supposed to be here at eight!

Cynthia (*aggrieved*) Oh! No-one ever told me.

J.D. (*teeth clenched*) I'm sure we did. Anyway – you know now!

Cynthia   But we're not all here, are we? Where's Robert?

Kay   He's got 'flu. He's not coming.

J.D.   We'll have to do without him. Mildred, you're not on till scene two. You'll have to read in for Robert. For now, you're Jeremy.

Mildred   Me? Read a man's part?

J.D.   It's only reading. Not much to ask, is it?

Mildred   Oh, sorry …   (*She enters from backstage.*)

J.D.   Mildred! You've just walked through the wall!

Mildred   Oh, sorry …

J.D.   Go out and come in through the door, stage right! And you come in immediately afterwards, Kay, from stage left.

Mildred and Kay enter from opposite sides.

Kay   You made it, then?

Mildred (*reading from her script in a deep voice*) Yes, I caught the three-fifteen train from Euston.

J.D. (*wearily*) There's no need to speak in a man's voice, Mildred. Just read naturally.

Mildred   Sorry … (*in her own voice*) Yes, I caught the three-fifteen train from Euston.

Kay   Is everything going to plan? You have the poison?

Mildred   Yes, everything is ready. She'll be dead by morning.

Cynthia enters, holding her script.

Cynthia (*dramatically*) You didn't expect me to turn up at this particular moment, did you?

J.D. No, we didn't You're not due on for another three minutes.

Cynthia But I always come on on page five.

J.D. This is page three! Go back!

Cynthia (*retreating*) No-one ever told me.

J.D. Carry on.

Kay I'm very worried about the whole thing. What if something goes wrong? What if she doesn't have her usual mug of Ovaltine tonight?

Mildred Trust me. Nothing will go wrong.

Cynthia (*entering*) You didn't expect me to turn up at this particular …

J.D. Not yet! We haven't had the quarrel scene yet.

Cynthia Oh – no-one told me.

She retreats, sits and studies her script.

Kay Of course I do trust you, Jeremy. Forgive me. But I'm so worried that *I* shall be the one to make a false step

J.D. No, no, no! Don't emphasise '*I*': emphasise '*step*'.

Kay How do you mean?

J.D. I'm so worried that I shall be the one to make a false *step*.

Kay Oh, I see … I'm so worried that I shall be the one to *make* a false step

J.D. No, that's not it – I'm so worried that I shall be the one to make a false *step*.

Kay I'm so worried that I shall be the one to make a *false* step

Mildred (*helpful*) I'm so worried that I shall be the one to make a false *step*.

J.D. (*glowering*) Just one director, please!

Mildred Oh, sorry …

Kay (*slowly*) I'm – so – worried – that – I – shall – be – the – one – to – make – a – false – *step*.

J.D.   That's it! Right – again, before you forget it.

Kay   I'm so worried that I shall be the one to make a *false* step.

J.D. (*in despair*) NO!

Kay (*bursting into tears*) I'll never do it! I just can't say that line.

J.D. (*wearily*)   It will come – hopefully before the first night!

Kay   I'm hopeless! I know I am! I'm just hopeless.

A step-ladder appears: it is being carried horizontally by Chris, happily whistling.

It's no good! I'm causing so much trouble. I'll have to drop out.

J.D.   You can't drop out a month before the play!

Kay   I'm so unhappy …

Chris   I just have to move that light up there …

J.D.   Does it have to be now! This is an important rehearsal!

Chris   Live and let live, old chap. You know what a stage-manager's job is like – and I've got to do everything myself. Now, let me see …

He turns round, the ladder swinging with him: the end catches J.D., who has turned away in disgust. J.D. collapses.

Now don't get in the way, there's a good chap.

Kay and Mildred help J.D. up. In the following, everyone speaks almost at once.

J.D.   I'm all right!. What the hell do you think you're doing?

Chris   That's right – blame me! I'm only the stage manager.

Kay   I'm letting everyone down. I'm giving up!

Mildred   No, you're not. The line will come.

J.D.   You're giving up! I'm giving up!

A moment's silence, as this sinks in.

Cynthia (*entering from the side*) You didn't expect me to turn up at this particular moment, did you?

SLOW CURTAIN OR BLACKOUT

Words, words, words
(A hitherto unrecorded event in the life of Will Shakespeare)

[This playlet was written around 1980, long before the popular film *Shakespeare in Love* was made. TAP produced it in their first Revue, **With a little bit of Luck**, in 1997. In 1999 it was entered for the Milton Keynes Arts Festival and won the award for 'Best dramatic scene', with commendation to the author.]

Characters

Will Shakespeare   **Bob Spry**

Richard Burbage

A room in a tavern near the Globe Theatre, London, about the year 1600. Will is seated at a table, pen poised over paper.

Will (*thinking aloud*) To live … ? Or flee the world … ? No, it sits not well upon the tongue. Two hours spent and still no opening line – words, words, words! Why have they forsaken me? In this play, of all plays! … in this speech, of all speeches!

He rests his head in his hands. Bob Spry enters hesitantly.

Bob   Master Will …

Will   What would you with me, Bob Spry? Be brief, I pray you, for 'tis a parlous time with me. I would fain pen a soliloquy, but nothing comes of it. And nothing can be made out of nothing.

Bob   I ask but a moment, Master Will. Will you let me, then?

Will   Let you what?

Bob   Why, play Sir Toby Belch in Twelfth Night, Master Will. You did say you would think on't.

Will (*wearily*) You are too lean, Bob. Sir Toby must needs be a man of girth.

Bob   Oh, I'll put on girth, Master Will, in no time at all – that I will. I'll eat and drink myself such a belly as will be girth enough for any man!

Will   Sir Toby needs more than belly …

Bob   Must Sir Toby belch then? I'm your man! You'll find none better than me for belching! I'll belch so that the Tower of London, no less, will shake to its very foundations! Listen!

He demonstrates.

Will (*reluctantly*) 'Tis a fair belch, I grant you, but …

Bob (*warming up*) Does Sir Toby fart too? I'm a rare one at farting! I'll fetch you such a fart as will echo from here to Windsor if the wind be from the east! Hark!

Will   Enough! He does not fart, neither does he belch. But leave me now, Bob, for I am sore pressed. The times are fraught. Our company faces a sea of troubles … (*he pauses thoughtfully*) … a sea of troubles – Hmm! (*He makes a note of this.*) Next week the Globe must close its doors for needful repairs and we must perforce ply our trade elsewhere in the city, which is not to my liking. But the devil drives – our coffers are all but empty. And I have yet to finish my new play. However, for your request, I'll consider further.

Bob   Thank you, Master Will, thank you! I'll be back anon for your answer.

Bob goes out. Will returns gloomily to his task.

Will   Death is peace … ? Death is sleep … ? To sleep, but perchance to dream … and what dreams may come? … Yes, that's good, for later in the speech … (*He writes.*) *To sleep, perchance to dream* … . But how to begin? Aye, there's the rub.

Richard Burbage enters.

Richard Burbage! How now, what news?

Richard (*waving letters*) 'Tis arranged, Will. Word at last! We are engaged to play next week.

Will   Against my better judgement, Richard. Whither are we promised? The Rose? The Swan? The Fortune?

Richard   Er – Northampton*.

Will   What?

---

* Change of name here is not recommended as this would destroy the pun in the following lines.

Richard Northampton, Will.

Will You jest, Richard! Say you jest, I beseech you!

Richard No, Will …

Will Is't come to this? What, are we strolling players? Or wandering minstrels? Oh, this is outrageous fortune! (*He pauses and makes a note.*) *Outrageous fortune ….*

Richard Did we not need the engagement, Will? And Northampton is, they say, a handsome town.

Will Cobblers!

Richard Will?

Will I tell you, 'tis a puny town of cobblers and other rude mechanicals. What's theatre to them or they to theatre?

Richard Come, Will …

Will Angels and ministers of grace defend us! (*He thinks for a moment and notes that down.*) Hear me, Richard, we shall want for audience. We shall play to the empty echo of our own words.

Richard You are too gloomy, Will … .

Will Marry, they will hiss us from the stage unless we offer nought but tumbling and low comedy.

Richard There you are, Will. An empty theatre cannot hiss.

Will And where in Northampton are we doomed to play, may Heaven preserve us?

Richard In the Town Hall.

Will (*pacing the room*) I like it not, Richard. I like it not.

Bob Spry pokes his head in.

Bob Well, Master Will? Do I?

Will What now?

Bob You know! – play Sir Toby.

Will Later, later!

Bob withdraws hastily.

Richard   Will, I have given thought to this matter of pleasing the baser members of the populace. I have heard that outside London they look more kindly upon a play, whatever it treats on, if it makes some reference in the title or the text, or better still in both, to names and places of the locality familiar to them. On hearing the which, it appears they do clap and cheer and fall about themselves in laughter.

Will (*after a pause*) Mean you ... to change the titles of our plays*?

Richard   Only a little, Will.

Will   *Two Gentlemen of ...* Northampton?

Richard   *Timon of ...* Ampthill?

Will   *The Merry Wives of ...* Wolverton?

Richard   *Othello the Moor of ...* Buckingham?

Will   But, Richard, if one particular is altered, then must others follow. If we play *The Merchant of ...* Bedford, Shylock must not make mention of the Rialto.

Richard   He must speak of what the audience knows.

He takes up a suitable pose.

        Master Antonio, many a time and oft
        In the cattle market you have rated me
        About my monies ...

    No?

Will   I like it not. And what if we present *Twelfth Night?* Give me Viola's first entrance, with the Captain.

Richard (*falsetto, as Viola*) What country, friend, is this?

Will (*as the Captain*) This is Newport Pagnell, Lady.

Richard (*as Viola*) And what should I do in Newport Pagnell?

Will   Aye, 'tis a question worth the asking ...

    No, it rings false, Richard! ... or if we play *Julius Caesar,* consider the confrontation of Brutus with Caesar's ghost.

---

* In the following sequence of titles, local place-names may be substituted, with care.

Richard (*as Brutus*) Speak to me what thou art.

Will (*ghostly*) Thy evil spirit, Brutus.

Richard (*as Brutus*) Why come'st thou?

Will (*ghostly*) To tell thee thou shalt see me at Bletchley.

Richard (*as Brutus*) Well: then I shall see thee again?.

Will (*ghostly*) Aye, at Bletchley.

Richard (*as Brutus*) Why, I shall see thee at Bletchley, then?

Will　　　No, no, no! 'Tis not possible. Must we sink so low? Must we pander to the unworthy? Must we grovel to the ignorant? Oh, in all matters today I am unjustly served! Wherefore? I am more sinned against than sinning. – Hmm! (*He writes.*) … *more sinned against than sinning* …

　　　Bob Spry bursts in with a letter.

Bob　　　Master Will! Master Richard! An urgent message has just come to hand – from Northampton.

Will　　　From Northampton?

Richard (*reading the letter*) We are not to play at Northampton after all. The Town Hall is wanted for bear-baiting.

Will　　　Ha! For this relief much thanks. Our company shall rest for a week and I shall perchance finish my new play.

Bob　　　But what about me, Master Will?

Will　　　What more, Bob?

Bob　　　You remember! Shall I play him then? Toby or not Toby – that is my question.

　　　There is a moment's silence, then …

Will　　　That's it! That's it!

　　　He walks about the room in great excitement and the words flood out …

　　　　　To be, or not to be: that is the question:
　　　　　Whether 'tis nobler in the mind to suffer
　　　　　The slings and arrows of outrageous fortune
　　　　　Or to take arms against a sea of troubles …

SLOW CURTAIN OR BLACKOUT

Murder in Milton Keynes Village

[Written while in Milton Keynes, about 1988. Not yet performed]

Characters

Detective Inspector Watson	**Constable Binns**	**Sherlock Holmes**
Mrs Sims, the daily help	**Mrs Hunter**	**Nesbitt**

The scene is a well fitted sitting-room, with doors to kitchen and to hall. Watson and Binns are discovered, pulling a sheet over a corpse on the floor.

Watson   You know something, Binns?

Binns   What's that, sir?

Watson   This murder is baffling.

Binns   I suppose it was murder, sir?

Watson   What else, Binns? There he is, lying on his face, with the back of his head bashed in. If not murder, then what?

Binns   Accident, sir?

Watson   How, Binns? Did he bash his head somewhere? Where are the signs? No trail of blood; no impressions on the carpet. No accident!

Binns   Suicide, sir?

Watson   Binns! Have you ever tried hitting yourself on the back of the head?

Binns   No, sir, can't say I have.

Watson   You're stupid, Binns.

Binns   Yes, sir.

Watson   Someone bashed him on the head. The question is, with what?

Binns   With intent to kill, sir?

Watson (*wearily*) The murder weapon, Binns. What was it? Where is it? Who used it?

Binns   We don't know, sir.

Watson   Thank you for reminding me, Binns. No sign of a weapon; no sign of a break-in. And who are the suspects?

Binns   Well, his wife was the only person in the house.

Watson   Fast asleep, she says, all night. After taking sleeping pills. So, our suspects are Mrs Hunter and – who? I'm baffled. I've been here twenty minutes and I'm baffled already. It usually takes much longer before I'm baffled.

Binns (*sympathetically*) I know, sir.

Watson   Binns! – Never mind! I've called in Holmes.

Binns   Who?

Watson   Sherlock Holmes.

Binns   You don't mean – the … ?

Watson   Don't be silly, Binns. He'd be a hundred and fifty years old if he was still here. It's his grandson, Professor of Criminology at the Open University.

Binns   I didn't know, sir.

Watson   The grandson has inherited that brilliant mind. He'll be here any minute. Now, we've checked all the windows and they can't be forced from the outside.

Holmes enters.

Holmes   Good morning.

Watson   Ah, Professor Holmes! Er – how did you get in?

Holmes   Through the hall window. They're quite easy to force from the outside. And you are Inspector Watson.

Watson   That's right, and this is …

Holmes   Watson! What an extraordinary coincidence – the name, I mean.

Watson   It's very kind of you to come.

Holmes (*looking at the body*) Not at all. I welcome the challenge. By the way, Watson, I sympathise with you for being called out on your day off.

Watson   How did you know it was my day off?

Holmes (*smiling*) Elementary, my dear Watson, as my illustrious grandfather used to say. You have not shaved. Why not, on a normal working day? No – you were called suddenly out of bed; you dressed in a deuce of a hurry, because you're wearing odd socks; and you were able to eat only part of a soft-boiled egg before leaving, because the rest is all over your tie.

Watson Amazing!

Holmes Now to the problem in hand. This man was killed by a blow to the back of the head, delivered, I would suggest, between midnight and three a.m., with considerable force, by a very blunt instrument. Do we know what that is?

Watson Not yet.

Holmes Who else is in the house?

Watson The wife, Mrs Hunter. She discovered the body this morning and phoned the station. She's upstairs, recovering from the shock.

Mrs Sims enters.

Mrs Sims Here, who are you lot? And what's happened?

Watson Police. Who are you?

Mrs Sims I'm Molly Sims. I do for Mr and Mrs Hunter. Here, what's that on the floor?

Watson How did you get in?

Mrs Sims How I always get in. I've got a key, haven't I?

Holmes I'll leave you to question Mrs. Sims, Watson. I shall take a stroll in search of the murder weapon.   (*He goes out.*)

Watson Mr. Hunter has been murdered, killed by a blow on the back of the head.

Mrs Sims Here, I hope it didn't make a mess on the carpet. Bloodstains are the devil to clean off.

Watson Do you know anything about this, Mrs Sims?

Mrs Sims I didn't do him in, if that's what you're asking. Mind you, there were times when I could've done!

Watson Is there anyone you think did have a reason to – er – do him in?

Mrs Sims   Oh, yes, plenty! Not exactly popular, Mr Hunter. (*confidentially*) The one you want is Mr Nesbitt.

Watson   Who's Mr Nesbitt?

Mrs Sims   Mr. Hunter's best friend, he was – except that he was having an affair with Mrs Hunter.

Watson   Are you sure of that, Mrs Sims?

Mrs Sims   Oh, yes – brazen about it, they were. I've seen it. They'd be at it upstairs, while Mr Hunter was down here watching snooker. He was snookered, all right!

Watson   Very interesting! Binns, go upstairs and tell Mrs Hunter I want a word.

Binns goes out.

Mrs Sims   Here, how can I do this room with that lying there?

Watson   All in good time, Mrs Sims. Was Mr Nesbitt here last night?

Mrs Sims   Couldn't say. He had his own key.

Binns returns.

Binns   The lady says she'll be down in a few minutes.

Watson   Damn brave woman, that!

Binns   Smashing figure, too!

Watson   Keep your mind on your work, Binns.

Holmes enters, carrying a tray with a large leg of lamb on it.

Watson   What have you got there?

Holmes   A large leg of lamb, wouldn't you say? This is the murder weapon.

Binns   You couldn't hit anyone hard enough with that. It's too floppy.

Mrs Sims   It was left out overnight to thaw. They was going to have a dinner party tonight.

Holmes   Consider, my dear Watson, what this – floppy object was like when it was first removed from the freezer. Hard, Watson, extremely hard! A most effective blunt instrument.

Watson   But that doesn't prove …

Holmes   I have examined it under the lens and found, not to my surprise, hairs – human hairs! I have no doubt they will be shown to match those remaining on Hunter's head.

Binns   Cor! Fancy being done in by a leg of lamb!

Mrs Sims   I always preferred beef, me.

Holmes   Mrs Sims, would Mr Hunter have used the downstairs cloakroom at night?

Mrs Sims   Oh, no – why should he? He's got an 'on-su-it' in his bedroom, hasn't he?

Watson (*puzzled*) 'on-su-it'?

Holmes   I know what Mrs Sims means. So – there was another man in the house last night!

Watson   How do you know that, Professor?

Holmes   The lavatory seat in the downstairs cloakroom. It had been left up.

Watson (*excited*) It was Nesbitt!

Holmes   Nesbitt?

Mrs Sims   He was supposed to be Mr Hunter's best friend. But he was more friendly with Mrs Hunter.

Watson   That's it, then! The motive, the opportunity, the murder weapon. You've solved it, Professor.

   Nesbitt enters hurriedly.

Nesbitt   What's happened? Why is there a Police car outside?

Mrs Sims   That's Mr Nesbitt.

Holmes   How opportune!

Watson   Mr Nesbitt, Mr Hunter has been murdered. We have a feeling you knew that!

Nesbitt (*staring at the corpse*) I – I – no – Dorothea phoned me – to come at once.

Mrs Sims (*helpful*) That's Mrs Hunter.

Watson   You were here last night, weren't you, Mr Nesbitt?

Nesbitt   I – I – no – I mean, yes, but …

Watson Mr Nesbitt, you came here last night, using your key. You paid a visit to the downstairs cloakroom, leaving the lavatory seat up. You quarrelled with Mr Hunter because of your affair with his wife, and in a rage, you hit him on the back of the head with a frozen leg of lamb.

Nesbitt No – I mean …

Watson Mr Nesbitt, I am arresting you on suspicion of murder. Caution him, Binns.

Binns (*uncertain*) Er – you do not have to say anything – er – if you do – anything you may say – I can never remember this new caution: it's much longer than the old one!

Watson Never mind, we'll do it at the station. (*to Holmes*) Well done, Holmes! (*to Nesbitt*) Wait for me outside (*as Nesbitt flees, turning back to Holmes*) Jealousy! The oldest motive in the game!

Holmes Yes. (*at the window*) Perhaps you should follow him. He's disappearing down the road.

Watson (*to Binns*) What did you let him go for, you idiot?

Watson and Binns dash out.

Mrs Sims This is better than watching The Bill! Still, must get on. I'm supposed to be doing the kitchen this morning.

Mrs Sims goes out to the kitchen. Holmes advances to the other door.

Holmes You can come in now, Mrs Hunter. I know you've been listening at the door.

Mrs Hunter enters, a handsome middle-aged woman in a dressing-gown.

Mrs H Professor Holmes, I presume?

Holmes Correctly! Mr Nesbitt is under arrest on suspicion of murder. That is, if they catch him.

Mrs H Yes, I heard it all. Poor Freddie!

Holmes Is he the murderer, Mrs. Hunter?

Mrs H If you say so, Professor Holmes. You're the criminologist!

Holmes It couldn't have been you, by any chance?

Mrs H   Why should I want my husband dead?

Holmes   I have a feeling, Mrs Hunter, that you were growing tired of both the men in your life. And lo and behold! You have rid yourself of both!

Mrs H   Can you prove any of this?

Holmes   No, and I do not intend to try. I am struck, Mrs Hunter, by your composure, your intelligence, your command of the situation, to say nothing of your physical charms. These qualities have quite captivated me.

Mrs H   Professor Holmes!

Holmes   My illustrious grandfather and my less well known father chose their partners with great care to preserve the unique intellectual inheritance of our families. I too must choose carefully. And I choose you. We would make an irresistible combination.

Mrs H   Professor, I hardly know you!

Holmes   You know my reputation. I have my idiosyncrasies. Like my grandfather, I play the violin incessantly. I take drugs, too.

Mrs H   It sounds exciting.

Holmes   It is. Will you take pot luck with me?

Mrs H (*after a pause*) On reflection, yes. I do feel drawn too you, Sherlock Holmes.

Holmes   And I to you, Mrs. Hunter – er – Dorothea, I believe?

Mrs H   Yes, Dorothea.

Holmes (*as they move together*) Dorothea Hunter, come to me. No, I cannot think of you as Hunter. What was your maiden name?

Mrs H (*they are very close now*) Moriarty! Dorothea Moriarty.

Holmes (*stiffening*) Moriarty!

CURTAIN OR BLACKOUT

Under Brickhill Wood
(a tribute to Dylan Thomas)

[Based on earlier ideas, this was written especially as the major item in TAP's Sixth Review in December 1992, to which it lent its name..]

Characters

Narrator	**Mr Compost**, a gardener	**Mrs Yacketty**
Mrs Chinwag	**Woman**	**Man**
She, a housewife	**He**, a visitor	

As with the original, this item is written with voice in mind. Other than a few hand props such as spade and supermarket baskets, it can be presented with the minimum of stage furniture. The narrator steps forward for his/her narrative and retires to allow the actors to perform their duologues.

Narrator In the Western shadow of Brickhill Wood lies Milton Keynes, the city that has no right to call itself a city: a national joke, renowned for its concrete cows, which few of its inhabitants have ever seen, and less well known for its two million trees, its lakes and open spaces, its varied industry, its Open University – the University with the invisible students – its pioneer multi-screen cinema, its indoor ski-slope and even enigmatic Bletchley Park. Here, in not much more than thirty years, three old towns and a dozen even older villages have burgeoned into a city of over two hundred thousand people.

Enough of history!

It is morning in the city. Milton Keynes stirs, fitfully, fretfully, frightfully, out of its collective slumber. The children awake from dreams of doughnuts and dolly-mixtures: the teenagers wistfully abandon their erratic visions of erotica: the businessmen emerge muttering from their profit-and-loss fantasies: the Councillors throw off their red-tape-tangled nightmares. Two hundred thousand dreams are packed away for the night and from Water Eaton to Wolverton, from Kingston to Crownhill, the city sits up in bed and braces itself to face the new day's challenge.

Before long, the so-called Streets (designated V for 'verticals') and the so-called Ways (H for 'horizontals') are awash with

85

the hectic, headlong, helter-skelter dash for the train that may not be running, or the parking-place that has already been filled: while along the Redways, the car-free, carefree ones walk, shoe-squealing, high-heeling, clip-clopping, clod-hopping, towards the stop for the bus that will no doubt be late.

Who else is up, early in the city? Let us meet Mr Compost, who moved from London's Canning Town where he had no garden, to Milton Keynes' Coffee Hall, where he has a garden for the first time in his life.

Enter Mr Compost, carrying garden tools.

Narrator Good morning, Mr Compost.

Mr C 'Morning.

Narrator It's going to be a fine day.

Mr C Yeah. Another day I'll 'ave to spend in the garden.

Narrator How is the garden?

Mr C Bloody 'ard work, I can tell you. 'Specially this time of year.

Narrator It must be.

Mr C It's back-breaking work pulling up all them weeds.

Narrator I'm sure it is …

Mr C And it's no joke pushing the mower up that slope.

Narrator I'm sure it isn't …

Mr C And the miles you 'ave to go to dump the rubbish these days.

Narrator The city is certainly growing fast.

Mr C It's not like the old days.

Narrator How did you manage then?

Mr C The rubbish, you mean? Oh, I used to chuck it over next door's garden.

Narrator That was handy!

Mr C Yeah, it were orlright 'til someone moved in.

Narrator Very inconsiderate of them.

Mr C   Yeah, but they never saw it that way. They kept on asking why their garden was two feet 'igher than ours.

Narrator   Some people!

Mr C   You've said it. Oh, well, must struggle on. No 'eart for it though. I don't know why I bother.

Narrator   Why do you, Mr Compost? Why don't you give it up and pave over the lot?

Mr C (*indignant*) Wot? Don' be daft! It's my only relaxation!

Mr Compost goes off, shaking his head.

Narrator   And there goes Mr Compost, retired and proud owner of a fine house and garden – with back-ache entered in the lease.

Meanwhile a new wave of movement stirs. Time for school, and from north, south, east and west, from all the Avenues, Drives, Mews and Closes that form the sinews of the city, emerge the children, the cheeky-chattering, satchel-dragging, hair-in-eyes, socks-at-half-mast children. Some walk directly to school, though more in these times are driven by anxious parents.

With husbands at work and children at school, a kind of peace settles over the city, which grateful mothers (those who do not also go to work) make use of according to their needs and after their fashions. For example, Mrs Bedbound of Bradwell Common, who has staggered out of bed in time to see her husband and children off with a yawn, then resets her alarm to 11.30 and returns to bed, lulled back to sleep by the sound of Classic FM, turned very low. Others indulge in a fine domestic, dish-washing, floor-scrubbing, bed-changing frenzy – especially the clean-living, clean-loving Mrs Everclean of Eaglestone, who, having dusted the budgerigar and polished the patio, pops off round the corner to vacuum-clean the play-area.

While in the shopping Centre, half-a mile long from John Lewis to Marks and Spencer, much of the mixed world of Milton Keynes may be seen going by, the short and the tall, the thin and the fat, the fair and the dark, the gloomy and the glowing – all different, but all with mobile phones at the ready.

At the nearby Food Centre, Mrs Yacketty and Mrs Chinwag, both from Tinker's Bridge, meet and stop for a chat in the middle of Sainsbury's, causing a pile-up of trolleys on either side.

Mrs C Hullo, Dora! Where've you been hiding? Haven't seen you for ages.

Mrs Y We've been on holiday, that's why – in Majorca.

Mrs C Oh, nice! Did you have a good time?

Mrs Y No,

Mrs C Oh – what a shame!

Mrs Y It weren't cheap, either, our hotel.

Mrs C Were you half-board?

Mrs Y Half bored? I tell you, we were totally bored! We've never been so bored on holiday. No-one to talk to – place full of foreigners.

Mrs C It's like that abroad sometimes, isn't it? Perhaps you should have gone B & B. You can eat where you like and it doesn't cost so much.

Mrs Y Wouldn't have helped. There wasn't a McDonalds anywhere. (*looking round*) Here, you get that trolley out of my back! No, we didn't like it at all.

Mrs C Did you go on any coach trips?

Mrs Y No, Jim can't go on coach trips, not with his bladder. You've not been away, have you?

Mrs C No. I like to go somewhere nice, but Trevor doesn't like abroad. He can't stand the heat.

Mrs Y That's unusual.

Mrs C Well, that's what he's like. He gets hot even in this country – overheated, like. On a warm night the heat just rises from him – you wouldn't believe it! Sets off the smoke alarm, he does.

Mrs Y Well, I never! (*aside*) Here, you stop pushing! There'd be plenty of room for you to get by if you wasn't so fat! The cheek of some people! You been keeping all right?

Mrs C   Yes, on the whole – well, bit of tummy trouble, actually. I get – you know – stopped up sometimes. Dr Harrison puts me right, though. She's very nice.

Mrs Y   I'm under her as well. But what about the new doctor, Dr Gordon, eh? He's a smasher! I'd rather be under him!

Mrs C   The things you say!

Mrs Y   Constipation's never been my problem. Regular as clockwork, me! Every Saturday night.

Mrs C   Oh! – Right!

Mrs Y   Yes, that's when me and Jim have our night out at the pub – a lot of beer, a lot of laughs, and when I get home – bingo! The night out does the trick, every time!

Mrs C   It brings out the best in you, like.

Mrs Y   You could put it that way. Here, I bought a nice top earlier on, Have a look. (*displaying the contents of her shopping-bag*) M & S!

Mrs C   Oh, that's nice.

Mrs Y (*reflectively*) Of course, I'll take it back on Monday – after I've worn it Saturday night.

Mrs C   Oh, you are cheeky!

Mrs Y   Why not? (*aside*) All right, all right, we're moving! – I must get a few things here.   (*She moves off.*)

Mrs C   Me, too. 'Bye now.

Mrs Y   Be seeing you.

Mrs C   'Bye … Oh, I've forgotten what I came in for.   (*She goes.*)

Narrator   … and Mrs Yackety and Mrs Chinwag go their separate ways.

A motorist visiting Milton Keynes for the first time drives three times round the Abbey Hill roundabout before going off in the wrong direction.

It has been statistically established that in a city like Milton Keynes, of every hundred families, three husbands will disappear after twenty years of supremely happy marriage, and will never be heard of again; five wives will abscond with other women's husbands; seven husbands will vanish with other men's wives; one long-trusted store manager will make off with the contents of the safe; one insignificant housewife will win £100,000 on the football pools with stake money owed to the milkman; and one small boy will get his head stuck between some railings, from which he will have to be released by the local Fire Brigade. All these things have happened in Milton Keynes – or will. It is only a matter of time.

Meanwhile, in the Caldecotte area, a different visitor, a lady, clutching a newspaper, hovers uncertainly before a house which displays prominently a banner bearing the notice 'HOUSE FOR SALE', and asks uneasily of a man standing nearby …

Woman   Is this the house advertised here in the Citizen?

Man   Looks like it, lady. You weren't thinking of buying it, were you?

Woman   Well, I was just thinking about it. It's a nice position, near the lake.

Man   Think again! Take my advice – think again!

Woman   Oh, well, I'd heard …

Man   Yes, you hear a lot of things about these houses – biggest con on the market! Here – tell me what the advert says.

Woman   Well, it says 'Modern detached house … '

Man   Detached! That's a laugh, for a start. Look how close they are together, these houses. I mean, you can't lean out of that bedroom window, can you? You'd bang your head on the next-door wall.

Woman   Oh …

Man   … and you wouldn't dare have a shower without drawing the bathroom curtains.

Woman   But – it seems so nice and quiet here.

Man   Ay, yes. It would be – except for the boilers.

Woman   The boilers?

Man	The gas central-heating boilers. Every now and again one explodes. It keeps you awake at night. People are complaining all the time.
Woman	Oh, dear!
Man	In any case, they're all on the move, you know.
Woman	The people?
Man	No – the houses. Soil creep, they call it. Every time it rains, these houses slide a few more inches downslope. In twenty years' time – mark my words – all these houses will end up in Caldecotte Lake.
Woman	I don't think I'll bother, then Thank you for your advice. Well – goodbye. (*She goes.*)
Man	Glad to have put you right, lady. All the best!
Narrator	Excuse me, sir. Now that the lady's gone, may I ask you … ? You seem to know a lot about this place. Do I take it you live here?
Man	Bless you, no. I don't live here. I work for Parkers, the Estate Agents in the City Centre. I've got three clients fighting over this house, and I'm not letting any private buyers get in first.

He goes off.

Narrator	In the more affluent areas of the city, like, for example, Walton Park, how does a bored, neglected, stay-at-home wife pass the tedious day once her well-paid husband abandons her for the dot.com world? Let us follow the progress of a stranger, male, well-dressed, dapper, debonair, brimming confidence, as he marches purposefully to the door of a Californian-type house and knocks [rings].

A man enters, knocks or rings at door, which is opened by a woman in a bathrobe.

Narrator	Such a lady opens the door.
He	Good afternoon, Madam.
She	Oooh! – aren't you handsome!
He	Is your husband home?
She	No, he isn't.

He   Ah! Does your husband leave you alone in the house for long periods?

She   Yes, he does.

He   Then I might be able to interest you.

She   You already do! There's no need to keep your foot in the door. Why not bring all of you in?

He   You're so kind. Tell me, are you bored? Does the day drag?

She   I've only just come out of my bath. Had you noticed?

He   Do you find yourself with time on your hands? And opportunity?

She   I only managed to throw a bathrobe round me. Does it bother you?

He   Do you ever have the feeling that you are just a caged bird waiting to spread your wings in a new world of adventure and excitement?

She   Oh, all the time, but especially now.

He   Do you feel there's a whole range of new experience you would just love to surrender yourself to?

She   My white flag is up already ...

He   Your husband need never know.

She   Who's going to tell him?

He   Do you feel there's a great void in your life and you're just aching for it to be filled?

She   Oh, fill it. Fill it!

He   Then I'm just the person you are waiting for.

She   You've convinced me. Come over here!

He   Excellent! Then let me explain our special privilege scheme for supplying this marvellous twelve-volume set of Encyclopaedia of Modern Knowledge on easy monthly terms ...

She (*shrieking*) Aaaah!

Narrator   And the lady vanishes inside, while the man crosses a name off his list and moves off to pastures new.

Evening comes eventually to the city. Children are fed, bathed, bounced and consigned to bed. Husbands return home with frowning bad-day-in-the-office faces, but are soothed by sustenance and the comfort of an easy chair. The city spends its evening in many ways, of which only some can be reported.

Walk through the dusk-descending city; look through windows; and listen. In some houses, the square-eyed willy-nilly, silly-billy telly, piping hot through the living-room wall, will consume the witless hours till bedtime. From this house, subtle smells ride the prevailing wind and denote a special meal for some special occasion. From yet another house, a sound of anger, voices raised in passion: is this real-life drama or maybe members of an amateur drama group rehearsing their lines? Through this window we see a teenager huddled over a computer. Is he furthering his education or merely playing games? It takes all sorts to make a city.

Some people are in the multi-screen cinemas, watching films to pop-corn accompaniment: some are even (to everybody's surprise) in an impressive new theatre: some eat their fill in restaurants: others drink in pubs. And at approximately the time that their elders quit pubbing, the young begin clubbing.

Midnight in the city. The street lights extinguish; the few remaining house lights follow one-by-one. Even at a late-night party, the glass-tinkling, crisp-cracking, dance-music-droning sounds eventually subside. The young return from clubbing, not always quietly. Silence settles over the city. For a few dark night hours, to the birds that wheel about the overlying skies, all must seem as once it was – before the city came to rest under Brickhill Wood.

CURTAIN

At the Restful Haven

[First produced by TAP as part of the second Revue, **TAP into Crime**, October 1998.]

Characters

Miss P, a prim lady   Mrs C, a Cockney lady

Grandma, a usually silent lady   Grandad, a doddery waiter

Mrs G, the grim proprietress   A man and a lady, would-be guests

Mr Jackson, a guest

The scene is the dining-room of the 'Restful Haven', a seaside guest-house. To one side Miss P and Mrs C share a table. The other table is unoccupied. At the back, Grandma sits silently staring into space. No-one speaks.

Grandad enters, carrying two plates with main courses: he is old and doddery and the plates clang together as he staggers in. He makes it to the occupied table, deposits the plates and staggers out again.

Miss P surveys her plate doubtfully, picks up her knife and fork, then discovers that they are chained to the table.

Miss P   Oh!

Mrs C (*confidentially*) They don't trust no-one 'ere.

Miss P   How extraordinary! You've been here some time, then?

Mrs C   Oh, I come every year, early in the season.

Miss P   So it's all right here then?

Mrs C   No, it's terrible!

Miss P   Oh dear. I saw it advertised in our local paper, in Cheltenham. It seemed quite cheap. That's why I came. I only arrived this morning.

Mrs C   They'd 'ave to pay me to come 'ere.

Miss P   But you are here!

Mrs C   Well, that's because they've paid me.

Miss P   I see.

Mrs C   I'm family, you see, and I 'elp out in the season. It don't do to 'ave an empty dining-room – puts off casual customers. That is, before the food puts 'em off.

Miss P   The food doesn't look very appetising, does it?

Mrs C   I wouldn't eat it if I was you. I 'ad some fish an' chips down the road.

Miss P   I don't think I'm hungry either. What shall we do with it?

Mrs C   Keep it for Bonzo.

Miss P   Bonzo?

Mrs C   'E's their dawg. Eats anythin'. (*shouting*) Bonzo! 'Ere boy! (*normally*) Come to think of it, I 'aven't seen 'im today.

Miss P   This side plate isn't very clean, is it?

Mrs C   Typical! I'd complain to Grandad if I was you.

Miss P   Is he the waiter?

Mrs C   You could call 'im that. 'E's family as well.

Miss P   He's a bit old for the job, isn't he?

Mrs C   Cheap labour! 'E's as deaf as a post an' all. Look, 'e's coming now. You tell 'im. – 'Ere. Grandad!

Grandad shuffles in.

Grandad   Eh?

Mrs C   You come over 'ere. This lady's got a complaint.

Grandad   Wossat?

Mrs C (*shouting*)   'Er plate. It's not clean.

Grandad   There's nothing wrong with the greens. – Awright, I'll tell 'er. – Let 'er deal with it … some people, always grumbling!

He shuffles out.

Mrs C   See what I mean?

Miss P   Oh, dear! – I do hope there won't be trouble.

Mrs C   Don't you worry. When she comes – 'er what owns the place – you tell 'er to 'er face. An' I'll sit back and enjoy it.

Miss P   How are you related?

Mrs C   We're sisters, really, but we don't speak unless necessary.

Mrs G enters.

Mrs G   Who's causing trouble then?

Mrs C   You've given this lady a dirty side-plate.

Mrs G   I might have guessed you 'ad something to do with it. It was clean enough when we set it. – 'Ere, you haven't been bringing in your own food, have you?

Miss P   Certainly not! – I …

Mrs C   Come orf it, Emma! It was like that when she came in. I noticed!

Mrs G   You would, wouldn't you! Well, I don't call that very dirty.

She takes the plate, wipes it on her apron and replaces it in front of an aghast Miss P.

    That's soon put right, isn't it? Some people don't know when they're well looked after. (*She looks round.*) Mr Jackson's not down to dinner yet, I see. Five minutes more and he's missed it.

Mrs C   Mr Jackson ain't well. I passed 'im when I was comin' downstairs. 'E was on 'is way to the toilet – if you'll excuse the expression! – clutching 'is stomach.

Mrs G   I hope he's not brought anything infectious into my guest-house.

Grandma (*suddenly breaking silence*) It was last night's beef.

All eyes are on Grandma

Mrs G   Oh, you've said something, have you? First time in a fortnight. What are you on about?

Grandma That beef you gave us last night.

Mrs G   What about it?

Grandma It was orf.

Mrs G   It wasn't!

Grandma Yes, it was. Smelt it the minute it came in. That's what laid Mr Jackson low.

Miss P Oh, dear!

Mrs G No-one else is ill. Who else had the beef?

Grandma Only Mr. Jackson and me.

Mrs G Well, you're all right, aren't you?

Grandma 'Course I am. Didn't eat it, did I? Had more sense.

Mrs G Your plate was empty, I remember. What did you do with it, then?

Grandma I fed it to your dog.

Miss P Oh, dear!

Mrs C No wonder we 'aven't see the poor little thing all day!

Mrs G If you've gone an' poisoned my …

She stops as she thinks better of what she was going to say, then runs out, calling …

Bonzo! – Bonzo!

Miss P She's very outspoken, that lady!

Mrs C That's Grandma. She's family as well – says what she likes – when she says anything at all!

A man and a woman enter hesitantly and look round. Mrs G returns and faces them.

Mrs G Well, what do you want?

Man Er – this is the Restful Haven Guest House, isn't it?

Mrs G It might be.

Woman We – er – wondered if you had a room

Mrs G I might have. Have you booked?

Man Er – no …

Mrs G You mean you've just walked in here off the street? We don't want no riff-raff in here.

The man and the woman look at each other.

Woman We've been travelling all day. And we just happened to see your sign.

Mrs G (*suspiciously*) You got luggage?

Man Of course we have. It's in the car.

Mrs G (*going to the window*) Is that your car, then?

Man Yes, the Mercedes.

Mrs G Ah! Well, I think I might have a room.

Woman We'd be so grateful. It's been a long day. And I would appreciate a bath before we eat.

Grandma Chance would be a fine thing.

Mrs G (*out of the corner of her mouth*) Shuttup, you old bag! (*to the Woman*) A bath? You've only just come!

Woman Yes, I know, but …

Mrs G Where've you come from, then? I like to have clean people in my establishment.

Man Don't your guests have baths here?

Mrs G They certainly do. Every Friday night, between nine and nine forty-five. Today's Tuesday. I'll go and see about the room.

She goes out.

Man Come on. We're not staying here!

Woman But I'm so tired, John, and it's getting so late. We might not find anywhere else.

Man Oh, all right! There's no way it can be as bad as it looks.

Grandma They'll find out!

Man (*giving her a look*) I'll go and get the bags.   (*He goes out.*)

Mrs C It'll be the fire-escape room.

Miss P I beg your pardon?

Mrs C That's the only room left – the one with the fire-escape.

Miss P I see!

Mrs C   In case of a fire, everyone upstairs 'as to go to that room, jump onto the bed, which is just under the window, open the window and get out onto the fire escape.

Miss P   What happens if there's someone still in the bed?

Mrs C   They get trampled to death!

Miss P   Oh, dear!

The man returns with two suitcases, which he sets down on the floor. The woman smiles wanly at him. Grandad enters.

Man   Ah – you must be the porter!

Grandad   Eh?

Man   Are you the porter?

Grandad   You want a drink of water?

Man   No! Look! Cases!   *(He indicates.)*

Grandad understands at last, sniffs, tries to lift the cases, but fails.

    Oh, never mind! I'll take them myself – as soon as I know where we're going.

Woman   Don't make things more complicated, John. Right now I need to know where the toilet is.

Man   *(to Grandad)* Er – the toilet?

Grandad   Eh?

Man   The loo, man. You must have one!

Grandad   Wossat?

Man   *(losing his temper and shouting)* The LOO!

He looks round, embarrassed: rightly so, since everyone is looking at him.

Grandad   It's closed.

Woman   What!

Grandad   It's closed at this time of night!

The man and the woman look perplexed. Mrs G enters.

    Can't understand these people. First they want a drink of water and now they want to go to the Zoo. At this time of night!

Man (*breathing hard*) Actually, we were asking about the loo.

Mrs G   Here, you haven't come in here just to use our toilet, have you? – because we're not having that.

Woman   No, of course not!

Mr Jackson dashes in, looking pasty and holding something behind his back.

Mrs G   You've missed dinner.

Grandma He hasn't missed much.

Mr J I don't really want any dinner. I'm not very well, you see. It's this ... (*He displays the cardboard tube of a spent toilet-roll.*) It's – run out ...

Mrs C (*cheerfully*) There are times when the most important thing in the world is a roll of toilet paper!

Mrs G   I don't know what you people do with it. I put a new roll in a fortnight last Saturday!

Mrs C   Never mind, Mr Jackson. Look, there's a public toilet just at the end of the road. You'll be better off there.

Mr Jackson gives her a grateful look, hands the spent roll to Mrs G and dashes out.

Mrs G   Don't take any notice of him. Riff-raff! (*to the man and woman*) How long are you staying?

Woman   Just one night.

Mrs G   Right. You pay in advance.

Man   What?

Mrs G   I've had people sneaking off early next morning without coughing up, I can tell you.

Man   Are you suggesting ... ? This is disgraceful! No loo paper! No baths except Friday! Pay in advance! Treating us like – like – (*words fail him*). Come on Jenny, we're not staying in this dump! I'd rather we slept in the car!

He picks up his two cases and stalks out, followed by the woman.

Mrs G (*apoplectic*) Well ... !

Miss P (*rising and lying guiltily*) Er – I've just had a phone-call. My – er – sister's been taken ill. I think I'd better go home. I'll just get my bag.

She hastens out. Mrs G is silenced for once. Grandad looks puzzled. Mrs C is grinning widely. Grandma's expression is unchanged.

Grandma (*after a silent pause*) Gone quiet in here, hasn't it?

CURTAIN

The Oldest Inhabitant

[Based on earlier material, and revived as another *Scene of Milton Keynes life*, this was the first of Pip's pieces to be read and produced by TAP in the first Revue, **With a Little bit of Luck**, in Autumn 1997. Changes to the location references would make it suitable for use elsewhere.]

Characters

The Mayor	Dorothy	Mrs Davis
Mr Davis	Mrs Lane	

The stage at a public meeting. The audience are the public. Mr and Mrs Davis and Mrs Lane are seated upstage. An empty chair is placed downstage C. The MAYOR stands beside the chair and addresses the audience. The time is the near future.

Mayor   Ladies and gentlemen, as the next stage of our celebration of the coming-of-age* of Milton Keynes, we are expecting a very special guest here tonight in the new Theatre Centre*, and I, as your Mayor, feel very privileged to be talking to her. We have sought out the oldest inhabitant of Milton Keynes, and with the help of her friends and neighbours – because, after all, good neighbourliness is part of the success story of this city of ours – we're going to get her to tell her story. By the way, she doesn't know it yet: she thinks she's going to Bingo, because this is her usual Bingo night, but the friends who take her are bringing her here instead ...

He looks offstage.

   ... and here she comes! Ladies and Gentlemen, a big welcome, please, for our oldest inhabitant – Mrs Dorothy Makins!

The Mayor ushers in Dorothy, who is a still-sprightly nonagenarian, flanked by her companions. The audience applauds.

Dorothy   Here, where are you taking me? This isn't bingo.

Mayor   Hullo, Dorothy!

---

* The event and venue may be changed to be appropriate to the performance.

Dorothy   Who are you? And what are all these people doing here?

Mayor   I'm your Mayor, Dorothy.

Dorothy   Eh?

Mayor   The Mayor!

Dorothy   You'll have to speak up. I don't hear as well as I used to. Here – you must be the Mayor, with that silly gold chain round your neck.

Mayor (*smiling*) That's right, Dorothy.

Dorothy   What are you doing here, then? You should be doing something about the buses, you should.

Mayor   Well, that's not really my job – but never mind me. You're the important person here tonight. Please sit down.

Dorothy   Eh? I may as well sit down. Not so good on my feet, these days.

Mayor   Good! Now then, Dorothy, how old are you?

Dorothy   Eh?

Mayor (*louder*) How old are you?

Dorothy   How old am I? I don't see that it's any of your business. I don't ask you how old you are!

Mayor   Dorothy, you're ninety-two years old!

Dorothy (*to her companion*) What's he say?

Mayor (*shouting*) You're ninety-two years old!

Dorothy   Well, if you know, why are you asking?

Mayor   That's just it, Dorothy. You are the oldest person in Milton Keynes. And all these people have come here specially to see you.

Dorothy   More fools they, if they've got nothing better to do …

Mayor (*hastily*) Dorothy, you moved into Fishermead* twenty-one years ago, in one of the first houses to be built in the new city. What was it like then?

Dorothy   What?

Mayor (*slowly and very distinctly*) What was it like twenty-one years ago in Fishermead?

Dorothy   What was it like? It was 'orrible! And it's no better now. It's them buses …

Mayor (*no longer smiling*) Yes, it was difficult at first. But fortunately, when things are rough, that's where good neighbourliness comes in. Do you remember when a young couple moved in next door?

Mr and Mrs Davis rise and move downstage. Dorothy notices them without enthusiasm.

Dorothy   Oh – them!

Mayor   Yes, Mr and Mrs Davis.

Mrs Davis   Do you remember, Dorothy, when I knocked at your door and said 'I wonder if you could lend us a little sugar? We're not very well organised yet'?

Dorothy   You aren't any better organised now.

Mrs Davis   They were good times really, weren't they, Dorothy?

Dorothy   I never did get my sugar back, did I?

Mayor (*hastily*) Tell me, Mr and Mrs Davis, what was Dorothy like as a neighbour?

Mrs Davis   Oh, she was wonderful! – Always lending us things when we ran short …

Dorothy   … and never getting them back!

Mr Davis   Of course, in return, we'd do little jobs for her.

Dorothy   What's he say?

Mayor   He said, in return, they'd do little jobs for you.

Dorothy   Oh, yes, like that pelmet you fixed over our lounge window. Came down two days later, it did, on my poor husband's head. Had to have seven stitches, he did!

Mayor (*getting worried*) Well, it's all part of being good neighbours, isn't it? Thank you, Mr and Mrs Davis. Please sit down.

The Davises retire to their chairs.

Dorothy   Can I go now?

Mayor In a few moments, Dorothy! A month or so later, another neighbour moves in on the other side of you – Mrs Lane!

Mrs Lane comes forward.

Dorothy I'm not speaking to her!

Mrs Lane Dorothy, this is your big day and I'm very happy to be part of it.

Dorothy (*staring implacably out front*) I haven't spoken to her for eighteen years and I'm not starting again now.

Mayor (*desperate now*) For years you lived in harmony with your neighbours …

Dorothy (*to the audience*) At least the Davises only wanted to borrow my sugar, milk and tea. She wanted to borrow my husband!

Mrs Lane Dorothy, of course not! We only used to sit and talk, those afternoons when he was off work and you were doing your part-time job at the supermarket …

Dorothy Talk, she says! My husband was a man of few words – the same few words mainly – 'Where's my breakfast? Where's my tea?' and 'Why don't we go to bed?' What he found to talk to her about for a whole afternoon I can't imagine.

Mrs Lane Well, I don't want to say anything to spoil your big day – though I could!

Mayor Now then, Ladies …

Dorothy She always was two-faced and I never liked either of them.

Mrs Lane Well!

Mayor Er – that's enough about the early days. Thank you, Mrs Lane!

Mrs Lane returns to her seat, somewhat ruffled.

What about now? What about the changes in twenty-one years? For example, how much did you and your husband pay for your house?

Dorothy What?

Mayor How much did you pay for your house all those years ago?

Dorothy I don't see as it's any business of yours – about ten thousand pounds, I suppose.

Mayor And what's it worth now?

Dorothy You'll have to speak up.

Mayor How much is your house worth now?

Dorothy I don't know, do I?

Mayor Well, I'll tell you. Your house is worth around eighty thousand pounds.

Dorothy What of it? I'm not selling it.

Mayor No, of course not, but it just shows what a wise decision you made. It was a good buy.

Dorothy Eh?

Mayor Your house! I said it was a good buy.

Dorothy My house what?

Mayor (*shouting*) A GOOD BUY!

Dorothy (*rising*) That's the first sensible thing I've heard from you. Goodbye! I'm off to Bingo!

And she goes, leaving a speechless Mayor. But maybe the audience will applaud.

CURTAIN

Quiet afternoon in Coffee Hall*

[Written in Spring 2000 for TAP, this was intended as one of the *Scenes of Milton Keynes life*, though it might reflect life anywhere else. Not yet performed.]

Characters

Gladys	Bert	The TV man
Mother	Woman	The husband

The scene is a living-room. Gladys is at the telephone.

Gladys Hullo? ... Is that you, Sonya? ... It's me, Glad. Just wondered how you were. It's my one day at home this week and I was looking forward to a nice quiet afternoon. So what's happening? I'm expecting the gas man and the television man. ... Well, the boiler needs servicing and the TV's playing up. ... Yes, they'll both come at the same time. And all I need is my mother to look in as well and chaos will be complete. ... No, of course I'm very fond of her and all that, but, you see, she's used to looking after quite a big house and this little sheltered flat she's in now, it doesn't keep her occupied, so she comes here and wants to run my house!

Enter Bert, who has obviously been painting.

Bert Is the kettle on yet?

Gladys Sssh! I'm talking to Sonya.

Bert It's all right for some!

Gladys (*into the telephone*) That's Bert. He's supposed to be decorating the spare bedroom.

Bert(*disgruntled*) May as well talk to myself.   (*Goes out.*)

Gladys He reckons he deserves a rest. He's been at it for fully ten minutes.

There is a ring at the door.

Hang on. There's someone at the door.   (*Goes out.*)

---

* or any suitable local name.

Voices are heard in the hall.

TV man (*off*)   Name of Jackson?

Gladys (*off*)   Yes, come in.   (*She returns with the TV man.*)

Now you're either the gas man or the television man or my mother!

TV man   I don't mind. I'll be anything you want!

Gladys   Cheeky! (*into phone*) He thinks he's housewife's choice, this one! I think he's the TV man, by the way he's looking at the set.

TV man   What's up with it?

Gladys   We get two channels.

TV man   Is that all?

Gladys   We get two channels – at the same time!

TV man   And you only pay one rental? Some people have all the luck!

Gladys (*into phone*) Did you hear that, Sonya? Laugh a minute, this one!

TV man   It's this cable service. When a set had its own aerial and something went wrong, all you had to do was kick the set and the aerial would understand. It would respond. But it's no use kicking the set when the aerial's miles away up bloody Saxon Street∗. Oh, well, better get my tool bag from the van. Back in a jiffy – bet you've never seen a TV man in a jiffy – ha-ha!

He goes out, pleased with his little joke.

Gladys   Yuk!

Bert enters.

Bert   Isn't it time for a cuppa? I'm exhausted.

Gladys   When I've made it, I'll call you.

Bert   Who said slavery was abolished?   (*He goes out.*)

Gladys (*into phone*) Yes, that was Bert. He's been painting for twenty minutes and he's exhausted. … What? … No, I won't hear a word against Bert unless I say it myself. Hold on – 'Housewife's choice' is back!

The TV man returns with his tool-bag.

108

TV man   That your old man I saw going up the stairs?

Gladys   Yes, what of it?

TV man   Pity! (*working at the set*) Well, I've got rid of your two channels.

Gladys   Good.

TV man   It doesn't work at all now.

Gladys   That is an improvement!

TV man   I'll have to bring you another set. Back tomorrow.

Gladys   I won't be in. My husband will be. He'll still be decorating.

TV man (*gathering his tools*) Just my luck! – I'm married, you know.

Gladys   It's not unusual!

TV man   My wife doesn't understand me.

Gladys   I've heard that before!

TV man   Well, she can't, you see, she doesn't know any English.

Gladys (*intrigued*) How did you manage that?

TV man   She's Spanish, you see. I married her on holiday on the Costa Brava.

Gladys   Well, well!

TV man   I got carried away.

Gladys   Obviously!

TV man   I got carried away by her two brothers. Seven foot tall they were! They caught us having a bit of – well, let's say a cuddle. So they carried me away – and her – straight to the church. Very strict, they are.

Gladys   You should have had one of those Spanish phrase-books with you.

TV man   Wouldn't have helped. Oh, well – '¡Que será, será!' – as they say. I'm off now, but don't fret, I'll be back tomorrow. ¡Adios!

Gladys   You should have learnt that word before you went on holiday.

She sees the TV man out and returns to the phone.

Hullo, Sonya, sorry about all that … What? … Tonight? No, I can't tonight: I've got something on. You'll find someone – there's always people glad of the money. Oh, NO! I can see my mother coming up the path! I'll ring you back. I knew it! I just knew it in my bones!

She hangs up and goes to the front door.

Mother! What a surprise!

Glad returns with Mother, whose eyes dart around the room.

Mother Just popped in for a minute – your path needs sweeping!

Gladys Does it?

Mother It's full of leaves and things. Where's your broom? It won't take me a minute.

Gladys Don't worry, Mother. That's Bert's job.

Mother Well, he's not done it, has he?

Gladys He'll get round to it. He's decorating upstairs.

Mother Your kitchen floor's all sticky. What've you been spilling on it?

Gladys I don't know, Mother. Don't worry about it. Sit down, I'll make a nice cup of tea.

Mother That's a big cobweb you've got up there.

Gladys (*patience running out*) Yes, I know. We're cultivating it – please sit down.

Mother Just let me run the vac up the stairs. It looks as if you haven't done it for weeks.

Gladys (*wearily*) I did it at the weekend. Look, Mother, I don't want you to do housework when you come here. Just sit down and pay me a visit.

Bert enters.

Look, here's Bert come down to say Hullo.

Bert (*ignoring her*) I don't think I'm well.

Mother You ought to sweep that drive.

Gladys What's the matter with you?

Bert I've got spots in front of my eyes.

Gladys   What have you been doing?

Bert   I've been rollering the ceiling, haven't I?

Gladys (*examining him*) Spots in front of your eyes! You've got paint spots on your glasses – from the roller. Why must you wear your glasses when you're rollering the ceiling?

Bert   If I don't wear my glasses, how can I tell where the ceiling is?

Mother   What about that cobweb in the corner?

Gladys   Mother, do me a favour and put the kettle on. Bert could do with a cup of tea. He's suffering from spots on the glasses.

Mother   I don't know what all that sticky is on the kitchen floor.

She goes out.

Bert   I've got spots in front of my eyes.

Gladys (*to Bert*) Now sit down and stop being stupid.

There is a ring at the door.

Come in! It isn't locked.

A woman enters, a little uncertainly.

Gladys   Hullo! You're not the gas man, are you?

Woman   No, I'm the sitter.

Gladys   The sitter?

Woman   Baby-sitter. Am I too early?

Gladys (*puzzled*) You're a baby-sitter?

Woman (*anxiously*) Oh, are you worried because you don't know me? I'm quite experienced really. I've done it lots of evenings since we moved here – except weekends, when my husband's home.

Gladys   Well, I don't know who you're supposed to be sitting for here. (*calling*) Mother, what are you doing?

Mother (*off*) I'm scrubbing the kitchen floor.

Gladys (*calling*) Make the tea!

Woman   It was arranged at the last minute by phone. I do a lot of sitting because – well, to be honest, I need the money. My husband keeps me a bit short, you see. Mind you, if he knew

I was doing it, he'd murder me! He's ever so protective – thinks I ought to stay home. Goes mad if I talk to another man.

Gladys   Well, there's clearly been some mistake …

There is a ring at the door.

Who's next, I wonder? Go and see, Bert.

Bert reluctantly goes off.

Husband (*off*) Is my wife here?

Bert (*off*) How should I know?

Woman (*in terror*) That's my husband!

Bert (*off*) Here! Who are you pushing?

An irate husband enters, followed by Bert.

Husband   So you are here!

Woman   Bob! I thought you were in Manchester.

Husband   You did, did you? Well, my plans changed and I've just got home. And where was my wife, eh?

Woman   How did you know to follow me here?

Husband   Your neighbour told me what you told her. Everybody seems to know where you spend your evenings, except me. What are you doing here?

Woman   Well, I'm …

Gladys   She says she's …

Bert   According to her, she's …

Husband   I can't get a straight answer out of anyone. Were you going to meet someone here?

Woman   I … I …   (*She bursts into tears.*)

Gladys (*intrigued*) You don't mean she came here to see my Bert? (*to the woman*) Tell, me, dear, what is it you see in him? I've forgotten.

Husband   Don't joke at my expense, Madam! – Madam! – is that what you are?

Bert   Here wait a minute … !

Husband (*pushing him away*) You keep out of this, whoever you are. You look as if you've come straight from work. Disgusting!

Woman   Bob, I'm only sitting in …

Husband   Sitting in! Is that what they call it?

There is a ring at the door.

Gladys   Come in! It can't get any worse!

The TV man enters.

Oh, it's you again …

Husband   So he's been here before, has he?

TV man (*jovially*) Well, I enjoyed myself so much when I was here last that I thought I'd pop in again!

Husband   This is a den of iniquity!

TV man   … and I'm coming back tomorrow!

Husband (*to the woman*) And you're part of this filth!

Bert   What are you on about?

Gladys   Shut up the lot of you! I've had enough! Do you want the whole of Sherfield Close to hear these ridiculous goings-on?

Woman   Sherfield Close? Isn't this Sherfield Avenue?

Gladys   No, this is 6 Sherfield Close. Sherfield Avenue is round the corner.

Woman (*looking at a piece of paper*) Oh, dear! I only wrote down Sherfield. I'm due at 6 Sherfield Avenue. I am sorry.

Gladys   I see it all now. We're always getting mixed up. We get each other's newspapers regularly and each other's post every time there's a new postman. My friend Sonya is at 6 Sherfield Avenue and you're sitting for her. I knew she wanted a sitter this evening. Look, Mr. Jealous Husband, Bert here – he happens to be my husband – he'll take you round to Sonya's and then you'll be satisfied that everything's all right And if you gave your wife more money, she wouldn't need to do baby-sitting. Now, for Heaven's sake, go!

Bert leads out a crestfallen husband and a still tearful woman.

113

TV man   Here, is it like this all the time?

Gladys   You chose a fine moment to come back, you did. What do you want?

TV man (*searching*) Left my screwdriver here somewhere – yes, here it is. Well ta-ra again. I hope it will be just as exciting tomorrow.

The TV man grins and goes. Glad takes a deep breath and sits at the phone.

Gladys (*dialling*) Sonya? … I've just sent your baby-sitter round. … Bert will explain everything. … It's been quite an afternoon. … Anyway, I'm going to put my feet up and relax …

She starts at an ominous sound off. Mother enters, operating a vacuum-cleaner.

Oh, Mother!

CURTAIN

Keep out of reach of children

[This was originally written in the 1970s, and was updated for the fourth TAP Revue, **Spring Fever**, in 2000. All the cast of children were played by 'elderly' actors, suitably dressed!]

Characters

Mrs Dale (A playgroup Supervisor)

The Children (Alvin, Jane, Elizabeth, Roberta, Mary)

The scene is set for a playgroup: a small table at the back holds mugs, a Ribena bottle and a jug with water. Elsewhere a painting-board and easel and miscellaneous toys and apparatus litter the floor. The stage is empty but children can be heard playing noisily off. Mrs Dale enters. She wears a white blouse above skirt or trousers. She chats to the audience while filling the mugs with Ribena.

Mrs Dale They're a noisy lot this morning. Five minutes more and I'll get them in. Lucky for me the weather's so good today. If they'd been in here all morning, making that much noise, I'd have an even worse headache. I don't think parents appreciate how much we playgroup supervisors suffer on their behalf. I must take something for my head. (*Rummages in a handbag.*) Where are those aspirins? (*Finds a carton.*) What's the most I can take? (*reading the instructions*) – two! – I 'll take three! – What does it say here? – 'Keep out of reach of children' – Oh, how I wish I could! (*Takes her pills with water.*) Right! Let battle commence! (*Moves to the door.*) All right, children, time to come in now!

The CHILDREN erupt into the room. Alvin whoops around, yelling 'I'm a guided missile!' Jane is crying; Elizabeth is silent and introspective; Roberta and Mary are fighting.

Mrs Dale Now come along! Alvin, settle down. Jane, why are you always crying? Roberta and Mary, you stop fighting at once! Elizabeth is the only one behaving herself. Now get your Ribena and settle down. You can play afterwards.

All the children, except Roberta, take their mugs and sit.

Roberta I don't like Ribena. I want coke.

Mrs Dale Hard luck, Roberta. (*to the audience*) Real toffee-nosed, this one, just because her parents are rich. (*to Roberta*) It's Ribena or water.

Roberta sniffs, but takes her Ribena. She sits with Mary and Alvin. They drink and talk. Elizabeth sits separately: so does Jane, who sips her drink between sobs.

Alvin We've got a new car.

Roberta (*sniffing*) We're getting a caravan.

Mary (*after a pause*) My Mum's got a shopping-trolley.

Alvin We've got two bicycles.

Roberta We've got two cars.

Mary (*after a pause*) We've got two dustbins.

Roberta We've got a O-pair!

Alvin What's that?

Roberta It's a French lady.

Mary What's her name?

Roberta Marie-Louise

Alvin That's two people.

Mary Is that why they call it a O-pair?

Roberta (*scornfully*) You're talking rubbish, both of you.

Mrs Dale Have you all finished your Ribena? (*They nod.*) Right! Mugs back on the table.

The mugs are returned. Alvin positions himself next to an unwilling Jane. Elizabeth sits by the painting-board and looks expectantly at Mrs. Dale. Mary and Roberta seat themselves at a box of building bricks.

Now, everybody, settle down to activities. Yes, Elizabeth, I know you want to do painting: you always do, but don't you start until we get your pinny on.

Mrs. Dale help Elizabeth on with her pinny. Thereafter Elizabeth paints randomly, but spends much time gazing at other happenings. Mary builds a tower of bricks, while Roberta watches in contempt. Jane is crying.

Mrs Dale Jane, whatever's the matter with you? (*to the audience*) She never stops crying.

Jane (*sobbing*) Alvin pinched my bottom.

Mrs Dale Oh, did he? Well, you can pinch his bottom – see how he likes it!

Jane No, I don't want to!

Mrs Dale All right then! I will. (*And she does.*)

Alvin Do it again!

Mrs Dale (*temporarily defeated*) Never mind him, Jane, he's just silly. Come and do some colouring.

Meanwhile, Alvin picks his nose and Roberta knocks Mary's brick tower down.

Jane (*sobbing*) I don't want to do colouring.

Mrs Dale What do you want to do then?

As Jane goes on crying, Mrs Dale has an idea born of experience and feels the seat of Jane's pants.

I might have guessed! Now off you go to the toilet and find some clean pants in the cloakroom. Next time, don't leave it so late. (*to Alvin, who is building a gun from Lego*) You didn't help.

As Jane goes out sobbing, Mrs. Dale turn to Elizabeth.

Mrs Dale What are you painting, Elizabeth? Is it a house?

Elizabeth thinks for a moment, then nods.

I thought it was. (*to the audience*) Whatever Elizabeth paints turns out to be a house. She'll paint a house anywhere. Last week she painted a house on that white wall over there – took me hours to get it cleaned off!

Mrs Dale turns her back to Elizabeth and focuses on Roberta and Mary. During the following dialogue her back presents a blank white surface, and Elizabeth proceeds to paint a house on it. Periodically, Mrs Dale senses something and scratches her back, but is unaware of what is going on. Eventually she moves away.

Mary She keeps knocking my tower down.

Roberta It was an accident.

Mary   Liar! You knocked it down twice!

Mrs Dale That's enough, you two! If you can't play peacefully together, go and do something separately.

Roberta disengages herself and nurses a doll. Jane returns, sits by herself and cries.

Alvin (*his gun complete*) Bang! Bang!

He dashes around, shooting all and sundry.

Mrs Dale Not so noisy, Alvin!

Alvin sits beside Roberta. Mary takes an interest in the following conversation.

Alvin (*to Roberta*) What are you doing?

Roberta I am nursing my baby.

Alvin   Why are you?

Roberta Because I'm its Mummy.

Alvin   Can I be its Daddy?

Roberta (*doubtfully*) I suppose so.

Alvin   Let's play Mummies and Daddies!

Roberta (*unenthusiastically*) If you like.

Alvin   What do Mummies and Daddies do?

Mary   I know! They go to bed.

Roberta Only in the night-time, silly!

Mary   My Mummy and Daddy go to bed in the daytime.

Roberta They must be very tired! Tell you what, Alvin and I will be Mummy and Daddy and you can be our O-pair.

Mary   I don't want to be your O-pair!

Mrs Dale (*sensing trouble*) Right! Stop whatever you're doing and gather round. Time for finger-play. (*Jane is crying more than ever.*) Jane, what are you crying for this time?

Jane   Alvin pulled my hair!

Alvin   No, I didn't!

Jane   Yes, you did!

Mrs Dale   When did he pull your hair?

Jane (*wailing*) Yesterday!

Mrs Dale   Well, it's too late to worry about it today. Now sit down, all of you. (*They sit.*) Who wants to do finger-play?

Children (*variously, except Roberta*) I do!

Mrs Dale   I'm glad to hear it, because that's what we're going to do.

Mary   I want to do *Five little Ducks*.

Alvin   I want *Old Macdonald had a Farm* – 'cos I like doing all the noises!

He goes through the repertory of animal noises.

Jane (*crying*) I don't want to do *Old Macdonald*!

Mrs Dale   What do you want to do, Elizabeth? You haven't said much this morning.

Elizabeth gets on her knees, puts one hand on her hip and holds the other out.

Right! We'll do *I'm a little teapot*. Are you ready?

Children   Yes!

Mrs Dale   All together now …

Children   I'm a little teapot, short and stout; (*They make themselves stout.*)
Here's my handle: here's my spout. (*They all put one hand on their hips and hold the other out as a spout.*)
When I see the teacups, hear me shout (*They all stand.*)
Tip me up and pour me out!

They all tip slowly to the side of the outstretched arm. Alvin leans so far that he topples on to his side.

Mrs Dale   Alvin! You've spilt your tea all over the best Sunday tablecloth. Now be more careful! Let's do it again – properly, this time!

They repeat the game as …

THE LIGHTS FADE OR THE CURTAINS CLOSE.

Family feeling

[Written for TAP's fifth Spring Revue, 2001, **Family Follies**. May seem reminiscent of a popular TV programme of the period – or even of more than one!]

Characters

Mum (old but acerbic) **Dad** (old and crotchety)

Aunty (usually asleep) **Millie** (mainstay of the household)

Jack (wage-earner)

The scene is a living-room. A TV set is placed downstage R, its back to the audience. A Sainsbury's carrier-bag lies behind the TV: that is, in full view of the audience. Seated LC behind a coffee-table are Mum and Dad. Aunty is asleep, next to Mum. Sounds issue from the TV. Millie enters from R and turns TV off.

Dad 'Ere, wot'jou turn that orf for?

Millie Why? You weren't watching.

Dad 'Ow d'you know I weren't?

Millie It was a children's programme.

Mum Well, 'e's in 'is second childhood, ain't 'e?

Dad So why was she watching as well?

Mum I weren't watching. I was far away.

Dad (*muttering*) Not far enough!

Millie Now don't start, you two. We're not having no rowing today. We had enough yesterday. And it's time you started talking to each other again.

Mum I ain't got nuffink to say to 'im.

Dad I don' wanna 'ear nuffink from 'er.

Millie It's ridiculous the way you two go on! Behave like grown-ups, why don't you, not like spoiled kids.

Mum It's 'im wot causes the trouble.

Millie It's six of one and half-a-dozen of the other.

Dad   It's 'er, ninety-nine times out of 'undred.

Millie   No wonder your grandchildren don't come near. They're too embarrassed. What do you think of them, Aunty?

They look at Aunty, who is fast asleep.

Mum   Sleeps all day, she does.

Dad   'Ow much longer is she stayin' 'ere? It was supposed to be for a couple of nights. It's bin two bloody weeks!

Mum   That's fifty pence, if you please.

Dad   Eh!

Millie   You know the rules. Fifty pence for a 'bloody', a pound for anything worse. I'm not having swearing in this house. Rowing's bad enough. But swearing I will not have.

Mum   'E don' know any other language!

Millie holds a box out to Dad, who reluctantly puts a coin into it.

Dad   Comes to somefink when you can't say wot you like in your own 'ome. What 'appened to free speech, eh? It's supposed to be every Englishman's birfmark, ain't it?

Millie   It's not your house any more. Jack and I pay the rent these days, not you. And we keep you, what's more. So what I says, goes.

Dad (*muttering*) No gratichude, kids, these days …

Mum   'Ow much you got in that there swearbox, then?

Millie (*counting*) Looks like five pounds and fifty pence.

Mum   Wot! That's since this time last week?

Millie   No, since yesterday morning.

Mum   Blimey, nearly pays the rent, don' it?

Aunty(*suddenly awake*) Oo-oo-h! I've got a terrible itch on my back. Scratch my back, Dora.

Mum   Oh, orlright!   (*She scratches Aunty's back.*)

Aunty   No, 'igher up – no, not there, over to the right – a bit lower dahn – more to the left. Oooh, that's better!

She returns to sleep immediately.

Millie   I'm going to get tea ready.

Millie turns to go as Jack enters

Jack   Hullo, love! (*He gives her a peck.*) Hullo, Mum – (*with no enthusiasm*) hullo, Dad.

Mum   'Ullo, Jack.

Dad merely grunts.

Millie (*at the door*) A bird's done something on your shoulder.

Jack   What? Where?

Millie   On your shoulder.

Jack (*annoyed*) Blimey! The town's big enough – why's it got to land on me?

Millie   You should keep moving. It's harder to hit a moving target.

Chuckling, Millie goes out.

Jack (*sitting*) How can you keep moving, when you run a market stall?

Mum   A bird's done somefink on your shoulder.

Jack   Yeah! Even the sparrows have got it in for me.

Dad   That's no sparrer. That's a pigeon at least.

Jack   What difference does it make?

Mum   Stop fussing. It's supposed to be lucky.

Jack   Lucky? Who for? It may be lucky for the pigeon – he's better off without it.

Aunty (*waking suddenly*) A bird's done somefink on your shoulder.

She returns to sleep immediately.

Jack   I know – I know! Don't rub it in!

Mum (*cackling*) Rub it in! Not likely! I ain't touching it!

Jack (*removing his coat and disposing of it off R*)) I'll see to it later. Right now I need a sit-down. It's been a hard day, even without the blooming pigeon.

Mum   Don' take it as a personal insult. Your Dad, 'e was just the same.

Dad   Wot's she on abaht?

Mum   Oh, yes, 'e reckoned 'e was a bit of a pigeon-fancier. If you ask me it was the other way rahnd. I'll never forget once we went to Trafalgar Square ...

Dad (*shouting*) Millie!

Millie enters.

Millie   What? I'm busy

Dad   Wot abaht a drink?

Aunty (*waking suddenly*) I'll 'ave a gin an' tonic.

She returns to sleep.

Millie   No-one's having anything now. We're having a drink with our meal, for a special reason. Anyway, we don't want you getting drunk again.

Dad   'Oo's drunk?

Mum   'Im – 'oo else?

Dad   Are you incinerating I can't 'old my drink? That's inflammation of character, that is.

Mum   'E was drunk last night when 'e come'ome from the pub.

Dad   I'm never drunk!

Mum   'E was drunk last night orlright. 'E tried to kiss me!

Dad   I tried to kiss 'er? Blimey! I must-er bin drunk.

Jack   Now leave it out, you two! I'm entitled to a bit of peace and quiet after the day I've had.

Dad   'Ow much peace an' quiet d'you fink I've 'ad with these bloody women at me all day? ... Orlright – I know!

He finds a coin and flings it at Millie's' feet. She rescues it and puts it in the box.

Millie   You'd have peace and quiet if you weren't so disagreeable. And at each other's throats all the time. I get fed up with it! (*as she goes out*) No wonder I believe in euthanasia!

Dad   Eh? Ain't that typical? Youf in Asia! Not a fought for youf in this country – oh, no!

Aunty (*waking suddenly*) Ain't tea ready yet?

Jack   Any minute, Aunty. You go back to sleep.

She does.

Dad   Bloody parasite, she is.

Mum   Millie! 'E swore again!

Jack (*grinning*) Lucky for you, Dad – she didn't hear.

Dad (*rising*) I'm orf to the only room in the 'ahse where I can get a minute's peace.

He departs, taking a newspaper with him.

Mum   That's got rid of 'im for 'arf an hour, thank gawd – especially with the newspaper.

Millie enters.

Millie   Where's he off to?

Jack   Gone to the loo.

Millie   Good. That gets him out of the way for the moment. You know what day it is?

Mum   I know. 'E don't.

Jack   What day is it?

Millie   It's your Dad's birthday.

Jack   Oh – I didn't realise.

Mum   Not that 'e knows it's 'is birthday, the dim ole git!

Jack   So what is he – eighty?

Mum   Eighty-four, more like!

Jack   Blimey! So he's not doing too badly.

Mum   That's a matter of opinion.

Millie   Anyway, I got him a little present.

Mum   'E don' deserve it.

Millie   Well, we always do – to show we don't have to row all the time.

Jack   A little bit of family feeling does no harm.

Millie   It's supposed to be a surprise, so I hid it behind the TV so he wouldn't see it.

She retrieves the carrier bag and puts it on the coffee-table.

Mum   Wot is it – as if I couldn't guess?

Millie   You know – the usual big carton of liquorice sticks. Keeps him regular, it does.

Jack   Once a year won't do much for him.

Dad (*calling offstage*) Millie!

Millie   What?

Dad (*off*)   I'm out of bog paper!

Millie   Oh, hell! I meant to get loo rolls this morning. It slipped my mind.

Dad (*off*)   Come on! I'm dahn to the cardboard!

Millie   The shop's closed now. Look, Jack, you nip down the road to Mrs King and see if she'll lend us a loo roll until tomorrow.

Jack (*reluctant*) Oh – I suppose so!

He moves to the door.

Mum   Mind them pigeons!

Jack   Ha, ha!   (*He gives her a look and goes.*)

Dad (*off*)   'Urry up. I'm desprit!

Aunty (*waking*) Wot's all the noise?

Millie   It's nothing.

Aunty returns to sleep. We hear a toilet flushing. Millie looks puzzled.

Mum   I dunno wot you got 'im a present for.

Dad enters, holding the newspaper.

Millie   Oh, you managed, then?

Dad   Cor! I never knew the Daily Mail be so 'ard on its readers. (*He sits.*) When are we going to eat?

Mum   Out one end, in the other.

As Dad glares at her, Jack comes in, carrying a Sainsbury's bag.

Jack	Oh, you're here. I got a loo roll for you, Dad.
Dad	Fanks for nuffink! Could 'ave done wiv it, ten minutes ago.
Millie	Now don't you be so ungrateful. He had to nip down to Mrs King for that.
Jack	And she insisted on looking for a carrier bag for it.
Millie	You know Mrs King! She wouldn't let you be seen in the street with a naked loo roll. Give it here. (*She takes it from him.*) Oh, it's the same bag – don't mix them up!

She puts it at the end of the coffee table.

Dad	I'm 'ungry!
Millie	We'll eat in a minute. Now sit down, all of you. (*Dad and Jack sit.*) Now then, my favourite father-in-law, what day is it?
Dad	Wot day is it? Fursday, ain't it?
Millie	Yes, but what date?
Dad	Date? I dunno. (*He looks at his paper.*) Fursday, May the fird.
Jack	Is that all, Dad?
Dad	Blimey, wot else? Fursday, May the fird in the year 2001 Annie Domino.
Jack	It's your birthday!
Dad	Is it?
Millie	So we bought you a little something.

She passes a carrier bag to him.

Dad	Well! That's a surprise.
Jack	Fulfills one of your needs, it will.
Millie	Well, have a look.

Dad looks inside the bag and is transfixed.

Mum	'E is surprised!

There is a pause.

Dad	Is this your idea of a joke?
Millie	What?

Dad   You fink this is funny?

Jack   What're you on about, Dad?

Dad   As if you don't know!

Dad fumes in silence.

Jack   Well, say something, Dad.

Dad (*suddenly exploding*) I'll say somefink! Oh, yes, I bloody will! No, I don' care 'ow much it'll cost me for the swearbox! I'm used to being pushed around but I don't 'ave to be insulted!

Millie   I don't know what you mean!

Dad (*removing the toilet roll from the bag*) This is wot I mean! Bloody insult, this is! Just wot I expect from this bloody family! (*tearful*) I live to eighty-four years to come to this!

Millie (*after a moment of dead silence*) Oh, crikey! I said don't get them mixed up. You've got the wrong bag. This is yours.

She passes it to him. Suddenly, everyone is laughing, except Dad.

Dad (*looking inside the new bag*) Oh! – You did this on purpose!

Jack   Honest, we didn't!

Dad (*grudgingly*) Oh, orlright, then.

Aunty (*suddenly awake and standing*) Excuse me. I'm going to the ladies' room.

Aunty takes the toilet roll and goes out.

Jack   Well – Happy birthday, Dad!

Dad grunts.

Millie   Let's go and eat, shall we? And have a drink on it?

Jack   Yes, come on, Dad

Jack leads Dad out. Mum rises to go, but Millie confronts her.

Millie   I want to know – did you switch them bags?

Mum (*with an enigmatic smile*) Now why would I do that?

She goes. Millie shakes her head and follows her.

CURTAIN

Mobile phone

[Written in Spring 2000 for TAP. Performed in the fifth Spring Revue, 2001, **Family Follies**. Ending modified in 2003 because of increased use of mobile phones.]

Characters

A woman	**A wife**	**Her husband**
An older lady	**A man** with a newspaper	Voice of **train conductor**

The scene represents a railway carriage in a local train. The woman, the wife and her husband sit facing the audience: the older lady and the man with a newspaper have their backs to the audience. They all rock to and fro with the motion of the train, to the accompaniment of train noises.

The woman takes out a mobile phone: the wife looks with interest, the husband with indifference; the older lady shakes her head; the man buries himself behind his newspaper. The woman dials.

Woman   Albert, it's me. … I'm on my way home, nearly into the station. … Yes, I know you're not expecting me until later tonight, but Auntie May was much better, so I felt I could leave earlier. … (*smiling*) You don't mind, do you – seeing a bit more of your wife today? It is my birthday, after all! (*pause*)

Albert, who's there with you? I can hear a woman's voice … What? … the radio? I can hear music in the background that must be the radio. … What do you mean, the television? You can't have the radio and the television on at the same time. … Are you sure there's no-one else there? … Albert, I distinctly heard a woman's laugh. Will you be honest with me? … (*with some anxiety*) Albert! … Albert! … Oh, he's rung off!

By this time, everyone else is interested except the man behind the newspaper. The woman dials again and waits but there is no answer: she looks anxious.

Older lady (*genuinely solicitous*) Are you all right, dear?

Woman   Yes, I'm quite all right. (*suddenly tearful*) It's just that he's not picking up the phone.

Older lady   Well, he may have had to pop out for a moment.

Woman   I don't think so. He's got somebody with him, I know.

Older lady   It's probably a neighbour.

Woman   No, it can't be. We don't speak to the woman on one side and on the other side there's a single man.

Older lady   It could be anybody from up the road.

Woman   We don't know anyone else. We only moved in two months ago.

Older lady   I'm sure there's a very simple explanation.

Woman   Then why doesn't he tell me who it is? And why doesn't he answer me?

There is an awkward pause.

Older lady   When you get home, you'll find that you were getting upset about nothing at all, you'll see.

Woman   I don't think I want to go home.

Older lady   Of course you do. Have you been married long?

Woman   Twenty years.

Older lady   Well, you can't throw all that away, can you?

Wife (*suddenly breaking in*) You simply can't trust them.

Husband (*embarrassed*) Here, steady on, old girl!

Wife   Twenty years, twenty months, twenty weeks, it makes no difference. You can't trust them!

Husband   We don't know the ins and outs, do we?

Wife   What's there to know? His wife's not expected home till later! He's with another woman. When she rings him, he rings off and then he refuses to pick up the phone. If that isn't proof of guilt, I don't know what is.

The woman bursts into tears.

Husband   Now see what you've done!

Wife   What I've done?

Older lady (*comforting the woman*) Don't take any notice, dear.

Wife (*relentless*) Has he done this before?

Woman (*in tears*) No.

Wife　　　There's always a first time!

Husband　Hey, come on! We don't know the other side of the story, do we?

Wife　　　What do you mean, the other side of the story? If I found you with another woman, there'd only be one side of the story.

Husband　You're always jumping to conclusions.

Wife　　　There'd only be one conclusion. You'd be out on your ear!

Husband　Well, you've never found me with another woman, have you?

Wife　　　No, I've never found you with one – but what does that signify?

Husband　What do you mean?

Wife　　　Majorca, last year!

Husband　What about Majorca, last year?

Wife　　　I never actually found you with that blonde tart Millie-whatever-her-name-was but I saw the way you looked at her.

Husband　Oh, come on! (*laughing it off*) If you're in a bar, you've got to look somewhere.

Wife　　　You were giving her the eye all the time.

Husband　Mind you, she did have smashing legs! Ha-ha!

Wife　　　You see? And how do I know where you were, or who you were with, when you said you were off playing mini-golf? Answer me that, eh?

Husband　Are you suggesting I was playing mini-golf with Millie?

Wife　　　No, I never thought that was what you were playing.

Older lady　　I don't think this conversation is at all helpful at the moment.

Husband(*aggrieved*) I don't see why you're taking it out on me.

Wife　　　Because you men are all the same.

Man (*suddenly*) I think this conversation is neither helpful nor in the least bit necessary.

130

Husband (*glaring*) Oh, you've come out from behind your newspaper, have you?

Man Well, frankly I'm fed up listening to all this talk, when it's got nothing to do with us.

Wife We're trying to be of comfort to this poor lady.

Man Well, I don't think you are succeeding.

The woman is now weeping copiously.

Husband So why have you put your oar in, eh?

Man I've not put my oar in.

Wife We've got sympathy for the poor dear, even if you haven't.

Man Sympathy my foot! Nosiness, more likely! You shouldn't have been listening to her telephone conversation in the first place.

Husband (*belligerent*) Are you saying my wife is poking her nose into someone else's business?

Man I'm saying that none of us should have got involved …

Wife Don't bother with him, Joe …

Older lady Really! This is getting out of hand!

Husband Wait a minute! I don't let anyone insult my wife …

Man I'm not insulting anybody …

Husband I've a good mind to knock your block off!

Man Oh, don't be childish!

Wife Leave it, Joe.

Husband (*shaping up*) I'm not letting him get away with it!

Woman (*suddenly*) Stop it, all of you! You're splitting my head open!

There is a sudden dead silence, as they all look at the woman. Then …

Conductor's voice Ladies and Gentlemen, we are now approaching Watford Junction. Watford Junction next stop.

The atmosphere subsides. No-one leaves, except the Woman. She is standing up to go, when her mobile phone rings.

Woman   Hullo! ... Lucy? ... Where are you? ... At home! But why aren't you in Canada? ... A surprise? ... Yes, I know it's my birthday, but I didn't expect – Lucy, were you there all the time? I mean, when I rang earlier? ... It was your voice? ... Oh, my God! ... What do you mean, you should have kept quiet? ... Why didn't Dad say it was you? ... And why didn't he answer when I rang again? ... Spoiled the surprise? You've no idea what you've spoiled! ... So why ring now when the damage is done? ... You thought I was upset? Too damn right I was upset! You've both made an utter fool of me in front of complete strangers! I've never been so humiliated – oh, never mind!

She rings off angrily and makes to go.

I wish I never had a mobile phone!

She leaves, with all eyes on her, as the train stops. There is a moment's silence. The train starts off again. Suddenly, four mobile phones ring, with different ringtones. The wife, Husband, Older Lady, and Newspaper man each reach for their phones. The following conversations all overlap.

Wife   Hullo, Myra. ... Yes, we're on the way, just passed Watford Junction. We'll be a little bit late at Euston – nothing new about that ...

Husband   Hullo, Fred! ... So Bottoms-Up came first in the 2.30! Nine to one – good for you! You can stand us all a pint on that ...

Older Lady   Yes, dear? ... We should be in at Euston in about fifteen minutes, all being well – though you can never tell, these days ...

Man   Hullo, Marjorie. ... Yes, all OK – no need to phone, really. ... Should be home a few minutes later than usual. ... Have the kettle on ...

There is a babble of voices continuing their conversations during the final ...

CURTAIN

Appendix

Items written especially for U3A casts

Appendix: items written especially for U3A casts

Note: the following are also especially suitable for older performers:

Watching the World go by (monologue – see Part 1)

Don't put your Grandma on the stage (choral verse – see Part 2)

Partners

[Duologue for elderly couple, written in 1999 and first read in a special TAP programme at an Activity Centre for Blind people, in November 2000: later acted in the fifth Revue, **Family Follies**, in May 2001.]

Characters

He **She**

He and She are seated on a bench overlooking a recreation ground.

She (*nudging him*) Wake up!

He (*waking with a start*) I wasn't asleep.

She (*pause*)It seems like only yesterday that we sat here.

He (*pause*)It was only yesterday – what are you on about? We sit here every day, if it isn't raining.

She   I mean, when we first sat here all those years ago. Twenty years ago, this month.

He   Was it?

She   Yes, we sat here and talked – about the new town, our new life, and all. We've sat here ever since, but we haven't talked. We've just sat.

He   That's true!

She   Not much use talking to you these days.

He   You don't talk to me, but you talk to everybody else. How come you talk to old Mrs Evans downstairs? You talk to her for hours.

She   Well, she listens.

He   No, she doesn't. She talks at the same time.

She   We used to talk a lot in the past. Tell you another thing, we used to know what the other was thinking. We'd sit quiet for a bit and we'd both come out with the same thing at the same time. Like …   (*pause while they think*)

He/She (*together*) 'Put the kettle on!'

She   Yes, that's right. That's togetherness, that is – or was!

He   Not much to talk about any more.

She   If I do talk to you, it's a waste of time. You're always asleep.

He   Who said?

She   Last night you slept all the way through Eastenders.

He (*indignant*) I did not!

She   Oh, yes, you did. All right then, you tell me what happened in last night's Eastenders!

He   Er, well, I – er – oh yes, what's-she-called, Tiffany, got killed in a road accident*.

She   There you are, then! That was weeks ago.

He (*grudgingly*) I may have missed bits.

She   You slept through last night's meeting at the Sally Army!

He   Well … some of those meetings are blooming boring, you must admit.

She   How would you know? You're asleep before they start talking.

He   Rubbish!

She (*waving*) Hullo, Miss Pearson! Hullo, Mr Wilson!   (*He waves too.*)

Look at those two, walking hand-in-hand! They talk!

He   Those two still walking out together?

_____

* This line may be amended to be appropriate to date of performance

She   They were walking out together when we first came here.

He   Twenty years ago!

She   … and they are still walking out!

He (*pause*) Do you think it's serious?

She (*pause*) Well, they don't laugh much – but they do talk.

He   Why do you talk to other people?

She   They're not asleep!

He   You talk to the dustman. You talk to the postman. You talk to the checkout lady at Sainsbury's. Now why is the checkout lady at Sainsbury's supposed to be interested in our last year's holiday in Majorca?

She   Well, it's good to talk! That's neighbourliness, that is. There's not enough of it these days. People ought to be spending more time chatting over the garden fence.

He (*pause*) We haven't got a garden fence. We live in a first-floor flat.

She   You know what I mean.

He (*looking into the distance*) Who's that, then – her with the kids? She's taking them to the swings. Crikey! One, two, three – seven of them!

She   And one on the way!

He   What's her name, then?

She   You know – Mrs Wellbeloved.

He   We don't see much of her husband. I never knew what he does.

She   I would have thought that was pretty obvious.

He (*pause*) What was all that to-do up the road this morning? Outside that new house at the end of the road!

She   Yes, I heard about that from Mrs Evans. They've just moved in. What did she say the name was? Began with a B … Oh, yes, Johnson. They've got a little girl – don't know what she's called.

He   So what happened?

She	Well, it was the builders' man – you know, from the firm that built the house.
He	What about the builders' man?
She	He'd come to inspect her frame.
He	He what?
She	The window-frame, up in the main bedroom.
He	What was the matter with the window-frame?
She	It wasn't square, or something. I don't know the details. I only know what Mrs Evans told me.
He	That doesn't explain the row, does it?
She	Well, it was her husband, you see. He comes back unexpected from being away on business and he hasn't got a key yet. So his little girl opens the door for him and when he asks 'Where's Mummy?', she says, 'Mummy's in the bedroom with the builders' man' …
He	He didn't like the sound of it?
She	He went up the wall, judging by the row. They sorted it out in the end, though. You wouldn't worry if I was up in the bedroom with a strange man, would you? You'd be asleep.
He	No, I wouldn't worry. You'd only be telling him about our last year's holiday in Majorca.
She (*pause*)	It's started to rain.
He	Better get home, then. Find something else to do.
She	You can go to sleep.
He	You can talk to Mrs Evans downstairs.

They move off together.

CURTAIN OR BLACKOUT

What's my Line?

[This sketch was written for TAP's fourth Revue, **Spring Fever,** presented in May 2000.]

Characters

Narrator   **Actors** (man & woman)   **Prompter**

Can be performed with a minimum of staging, so long as there are suitable pieces of furniture to hold the magazine and newspaper – in different places.

Narrator (*entering and coming downstage*) Every performer, in whatever field of the performing arts, has a recurrent nightmare, a dread that something will go horribly wrong during a performance – the solo violinist fears that a string will break half-way through a daunting cadenza: the principal soprano dreads the possibility that she will not make that ultimate top 'E'!

And in the field of Theatre, what the actor dreads is 'drying' – that is, bringing the play to a standstill by forgetting the next line. There are several possible reasons for drying. It could be stage-fright or a lapse in concentration – caused maybe by a prop in the wrong place, or even missing altogether. Or, in the case of ageing Thespians like us, it might be that they have difficulty in learning the lines in the first place, or in remembering them afterwards!

But drying is not a problem peculiar to amateur theatre. It can happen in the professional theatre too, even in London's West End. Is there a solution to this problem? Yes, of course there is, and it's called 'the Prompter'.

The Prompter enters L and stands awaiting instructions.

(*indicating*) There (s)he is! The prompter is usually an actor who hasn't landed a part. Traditionally he or she sits offstage left – that is, actors' left – just behind the curtain and thus invisible to the audience. But we will let you see our prompter for the purpose of illustration.

The Prompter sits on a chair L, clutching scripts.

The prompter hugs the script, follows the action, and when needed, supplies the next line, in a voice that carries to the actor – but not, of course, to the audience! Let's bring on a

couple of actors so that you can see how the system works –
or sometimes doesn't!

The Man and Woman enter R and remain facing each other RC.

Some action, please!

Woman   Gordon! What are you doing here?

Man   I – er ... (*then blank*)

Narrator (*to audience*) Gordon has 'dried'. He waits for a prompt.

Prompter (*whispering*) I've come for my share of the money.

... *but not even the actor can hear him/her!*

Narrator   The prompt is too soft.

The Man looks appealingly to L.

Prompter (*slightly louder*) I've come for my share of the money.

The man looks horrified.

Narrator   He (she) is still too soft.

The Man crosses to L looking daggers at the Prompter. Eventually he resorts to bending down near Prompter and pretending to tie his shoelace.

Man (*in stage whisper*) I can't bloody hear!

Prompter (*loudly*) I've come for my share of the money.

Narrator   This is just as confusing for the audience – it sounds like
another actor offstage, so why doesn't he come on?

The Man returns to face the Woman RC.

So the prompter may be either too loud or too soft – or even
too slow or too quick!

Woman   Gordon! What are you doing here?

Man   Aha!   (*strikes a dramatic pose, pointing at the Woman.*)

Prompter (*not understanding*) I've come for my share of the money.

The Man looks furiously at the Prompter.

Narrator   No wonder he's annoyed! That was too quick and not
necessary: the actor was pausing for dramatic effect.

Prompters, like other people, are prone to human failings! Let's try again!

The Prompter starts to doze.

Woman Gordon! What are you doing here?

Man I – er … (*then blank.*   *The prompter is dozing.*)

Narrator The Prompter has fallen asleep.

The Man and the Woman look helplessly at the Prompter, who is snoring

This occasionally happens if the play so far is very boring. (*meaningfully*) It can happen to the audience too, of course!

Another danger arises when the programme consists of several items, for example a trio of one-act plays, or a series of sketches in a revue. A prompter who is not quite up to the job may get his scripts mixed up.

Prompter wakes up and begins to sort pages.

Woman Gordon! What are you doing here?

Man I – er … (*then blank, as before, glares at Prompter.*)

Prompter, panic-stricken, hastily shuffles through pages of script.

Narrator Eventually, in despair, the actor falls back on a last resort – and this has been done at any level of theatre! He demands a prompt.

Man (*striding over to L*) What's the line?

Prompter (*still turning over pages*) What's the sketch?

Narrator There is another 'trick of the trade' that is widely used if the Prompter is unreliable, or not available for some reason.

Prompter goes offstage L.

The device is to have little bits of script scattered at strategic locations on the stage to help out at difficult moments. This is especially useful when actors are prone to 'dry' on particular cues. After all, what is more natural than that in the course of conversation someone wanders round the room, glances at a newspaper on a chair, or a letter on a desk, or casually picks up a magazine from the coffee-table? We have arranged for all this to be in place so that you can see how it works!

Woman   Gordon! What are you doing here?

Man   I – er … (*then blank., as before.*)

The Man, stumped, wanders about the stage, picks up a magazine and casually glances at it. His face clears.

Man   I like jelly and custard. I've always liked jelly and custard.

Both Man and woman stop in their tracks, aghast!

Narrator   Ah! You can see what went wrong there, can't you? He's picked up the wrong crib. The correct line for this scene is stuck inside the newspaper: the line in the magazine belongs to the second act.

Some Companies will not have a prompter. If an actor dries, then it is up to him or her and whoever else is on stage at the time to sort it out. Of course, an actor who dries in the middle of a Shakespearean soliloquy is in dire trouble! But this is rare: it is more likely in a modern play with everyday dialogue. In the absence of the correct line, an actor can ad lib until something sparks off the required words. But not all actors are good at ad-libbing. It could go something like this:

Woman   Gordon! What are you doing here?

Man (*floundering*) I – er … How are you?

Woman   I'm fine – but what are you doing here?

Man (*seeking inspiration*) How's your mother?

Woman (*gritting her teeth*) She's well, thank you, but (*loudly*) What are you …

Man   … and your father?

Woman (*thinking hard*) Gordon, he died, leaving me all that money!

Man   Oh, I am so sorry …

Woman   You knew about it months ago. But (*intensely*) why are you here?

Man   Well, (*desperately*) I live here – don't I?

Woman (*hissing*) Gordon, you haven't lived here for twelve years. You left me! Remember?

Man   Oh … (*speechless*)

Woman (*seeing a way out*) You don't think you're going to get any of what Dad left me, do you?

Man (*delighted*) Yes, that's it. I've come for my share of the money.

Narrator So you see, they manage to get round to the required line – eventually! Mind you, too much ad-libbing does tend to lengthen a play!

So ends our examination of the actor's nightmare. If you ever ... (*dries*)

Prompter enters L.

Prompter ... if you ever watch an actor 'dry' ...

Narrator (*gratefully*) If you ever watch an actor 'dry', be sympathetic! You see, the system does work – sometimes!

CURTAIN OR BLACKOUT

The new member

[This parody was written in 2001 and performed as a TAP contribution to Milton Keynes U3A's Jubilee show, **Jubilations**, in 2002. It is also suitable for other Companies or Play Festivals, with the inclusion of a suitable Prologue and/or Programme note.]

Prologue (*optional, for audiences not familiar with U3A*)

> This playlet was written for performance for the University of the Third Age, the international organisation for active retired people. As well as supporting various active interest groups, U3As usually have a monthly open meeting with a visiting speaker, the larger numbers requiring a local hall to be hired from another organisation, such as the Salvation Army.

Characters

Kate (practical)   **Janice** (*nervous*)   **Alison** (*musical*)

Marjorie (robust, active)   **Penelope** (*dramatic*)

> *Curtains open on the foyer of a Community meeting venue: some Salvation Army notices are visible. Kate is seated at a table facing the street entrance, counting the takings. Behind her is the exit to the meeting hall.*

Kate   Hmmm! Not many today!

Janice enters, very tentatively.

>   Hullo!

Janice (*nervous*) Oh – hullo! This is the Salvation Army Hall, isn't it?

Kate   It certainly is. You've missed the talk, I'm afraid.

Janice   Oh, I didn't know there were talks.

Kate   Oh, yes, always on the last Wednesday of every month. There's probably some tea going.

Janice   Er – No, thank you. – I've only come to join, you see.

Kate   Oh! Great – a new member! You're very welcome.

>   *Alison enters.*

>   Alison! We have a new member.

144

Alison   Oh good! We're always glad of new members. We're a bit short on the ground these days.

Janice   Really? I wouldn't have thought …

Kate   I'll leave you with Ali for the moment. I need to have a word with Martin in there. (*as she goes*) What did you say your name was? Never mind, write it down there, with your address and phone number. I'm Kate, by the way.

As Janice writes, Kate leaves.

Alison   So you've come to join us. Jolly good! There's lots you can do – er – (*looking at the paper*) Janice. But tell me, how do you feel about singing?

Janice   Oh, yes, that's one of the things I've been looking forward to.

Alison   That's splendid! I'm so glad to hear it! I look after the singing, you see. What are you – soprano? Contralto?

Janice   Er – I'm not sure, actually …

Alison   Never mind, we'll soon sort you out. Look, why don't you sing something for me now?

Janice   Well – what shall I sing?

Alison   Anything you like! Folk, blues – operatic aria! No, just kidding! Absolutely anything.

Janice sings: it is not very good. Alison winces. Janice stops.

Alison   Well! … There's a lot of promise there. It can only get better. That's why we rehearse regularly.

Janice   You rehearse?

Alison   Oh, yes. We have to get it right – not that we always do, but we try! No, actually, I'm kidding. People tell us we're really quite good.

Marjorie enters.

(*change of tone*) What are you doing here?

Marjorie   (*ignoring her*) So we have a new member! The jungle telegraph never fails. I'm Marjorie, but everyone calls me Marj. You are … ?

Janice   Er – Janice.

Marjorie   Well, Janice, we're always on the lookout for new active members.

Alison   I've already told her that!

Marjorie   I'm in charge of Movement to Music.

Alison   Janice is more interested in singing.

Janice   Oh, no, I …

Marjorie   That's all right. Room for both.

Alison   We don't like to overload new members.

Marjorie (*turning to Alison*) Look, Ali, you know we're short of active members.

Alison   So are we!

Marjorie   We're just two bodies short of an eightsome reel.

Alison   Our need is greater than yours.

Janice   Er – I always thought that the music and the movement went together.

Marjorie   They do! They do! You have exactly the right approach, Janice.

Alison (*hissing, aside*) I saw her first.

Marjorie (*ignoring her*) You take care of the body at the same time as you're enjoying the music.

Janice   Yes, but …

Marjorie   It does wonders for your fitness. You look in good shape to me, Janice. Why don't we try a little movement together? Can you do this?   (*She pirouettes.*)

Janice   Well, yes, I think I can …   (*She does, rather uncertainly.*)

Marjorie   That's good!

Janice   … but I don't quite understand …

Alison (*to Marjorie*) You only do Movement to Music to keep your weight down.

Marjorie   I don't need to keep my weight down!

Alison   Yes, you do! You're fat!

Marjorie Me? Fat!

Alison Yes, fat! That goes for the lot of you!

Marjorie Hark who's talking! You string a couple of notes together and you think you're Maria bloody Callas!

Janice (*bewildered*) Really! There's no need to …

She looks round as Penelope enters, with a flourish..

Penelope (*dramatically*) What's this I see? A new face?

Alison Not her as well!

Penelope A new arrival! How timely! Just what the doctor ordered. I'm Penelope – Third-Age Players! You are … ?

Janice Janice – but I don't understand …

Penelope We're always on the lookout for new members.

Marjorie She knows that!

Penelope Shush a minute! (*to Janice*) Say something!

Janice Well, really, I'm a bit bewildered …

Penelope But that's simply marvellous! Diction as clear as a bell. Honestly, darling, you're a natural for our group. You're just the sort of person we want. What did you say your name was?

Janice Janice, but I'm not sure …

Penelope Delighted to welcome you on board, Janice. You won't regret it, darling, I promise! You don't mind if I call you darling, do, you, darling? We all call each other darling, even thought we hate everyone like poison, especially the ones who get the best parts.

Alison Stop acting, Penny!

Penelope (*ignoring her*) Actually, we're doing a play at the moment. – Golly! Why has it only just occurred to me? You wouldn't like a part, would you? Someone's just dropped out.

Marjorie Penny, it isn't right to rush Janice into anything …

Alison That's what you were doing.

Marjorie I was not!

Penelope No-one's rushing her, darling. It's entirely up to her. It would be absolutely marvellous if you could take over this part. Of course, the play's going on next week, so you'll have to learn your lines …

Marjorie That would be a novelty!

Penelope Take no notice, Janice. We're a jolly good group. One thing about us, you don't have to sleep with the director to land a part – we're past all that! Actually, the director's a woman. Unfortunately we haven't had a man in the group for years.

Alison That's no surprise.

Marjorie There aren't any men in your group either.

Alison Oh, shut up, Fat!

Marjorie Don't you call me that!

Marjorie wallops Alison.

Alison Fat cow!

Alison wallops Marjorie.

Penelope Just ignore them, Janice. Now it so happens that I have a couple of scripts with me, so we could go over one of the scenes. This one will do. You are the Grand Duchess of Montevosnia, and I'll read Tatiana, who is your grand-niece – er – Janice?

But Janice is watching in amazement as Alison and Marjorie are locked in mortal combat.

Never mind those two. They're really the best of friends.

Kate enters, aghast.

Kate For Heaven's sake! What on earth … ?

All speak rapidly, overlapping each other:

Penelope I'm trying to rehearse a scene!

Alison She's an interfering cow!

Marjorie She ought to be thrown out!

Janice (*at last asserting herself*) PLEASE! May I say something? I don't understand what's going on here. And I don't understand why you're not all in uniform.

All the others (*severally*) Uniform?

Janice   Well, yes – I'm here to join the Salvation Army.

They all stare at her.

CURTAIN OR BLACKOUT

The Wine–tasters

[This sketch was written at the end of 1999, especially for the U3A Millennium party. It could be performed by other Companies or Play Festivals, with changes of event and the 'vintages', and the inclusion of a suitable Prologue and/or Programme note.]

Prologue (*optional, for audiences not familiar with U3A*)

> This playlet was written for performance for the University of the Third Age, the international organisation for active retired people. Wine-tasting is often one of the various local group activities.

Characters

Dudley (pompous) **Fred** (coarse) **Glad** (his unhappy wife)

Penelope (prim and proper) **Gloria** (not too bright) **Delia** (very quiet)

The scene is a room, with a table set for six places: Dudley is at the end, R, Penelope at the end L, and between them, right to left, Delia, Gloria, Glad and Fred. There are four wine bottles on the table. There is general chatter.

Dudley (*coughing to attract attention*) Well, ladies and gentlemen – gentleman I should say – we've chatted long enough, now down to business.

Penelope (*severely*) About time!

Dudley (*ignoring her*) May I, as your chairman, welcome you all to what will be the last meeting of the Wine Appreciation Group this year, indeed, this century, and even this millennium. When we've done our tasting, if there's any wine left over, we'll drink to the future.

Gloria There's always some left over.

Fred And we always drink it up. Ha, ha!

Glad You drink most of it.

Fred (*aggrieved*) I do not! Anyway, we can't waste it.

Dudley Well, I can fetch out another bottle or two if need be. It's a little unfortunate that we don't have our full membership this afternoon …

Fred   That's a good thing! There'll be more for us to drink. Ha, ha!

Glad   Pig!

Penelope Sometimes drinking up what's left in all the bottles can have unfortunate consequences. Does anyone remember what happened after our last meeting when we finished up all the bottles?

The others look blank.

Dudley   No, I can't say I do.

Penelope Several people were arrested for riotous behaviour.

The all look at Fred. Delia gets up abruptly.

Delia   Excuse me.

Delia leaves the room: the others gaze after her.

Dudley   Already?

Fred   She can't hold it, you know.

Dudley   But we haven't started tasting yet.

Gloria   It's just the thought of it sets her off.

Penelope Ridiculous!

Dudley   We must press on regardless. This afternoon we are considering four local wines which, I understand, are becoming quite popular.

Delia returns.

Gloria   Better now, dear?   (*Delia smiles wanly and sits.*)

Dudley   Please have your glasses ready.

All bring out wine glasses, except Fred, who brings out a tankard. The others look at him.

Fred   My taste-buds react very slow.

Glad   Pig!

Fred (*ignoring her*) Before we start – do we have to spit?

Penelope Of course! It's the done thing.

Gloria   I think spitting's rude.

Glad   Well, it is a bit wasteful.

Dudley (*resigned*) This comes up every time we meet. We'll put it to the vote. Those in favour of spitting?

Dudley and Penelope raise their hands.

Those against?

Fred, Gloria and Glad raise their hands, then Delia follows suit.

Well, then we don't spit. Let's get on. The first wine we sample is a red – *Domaine Vieux Manoir de* Newport Pagnell 1998.

Fred puts a cigarette in his mouth and prepares to use a lighter. The others look at him. He stops.

Er – Fred, we don't smoke, do we! It could affect our tasting.

Fred   Sorry, I forgot.

Glad   You always forget.

Penelope Disgusting!

Dudley   Shall we taste?

The bottle is passed round: each pours a little, except Fred, who pours a lot. Some drink. Penelope sniffs.

Penelope What do you think of the aroma?

Dudley (*sniffing*) The aroma?

Penelope There's a distinct hint of – petrol.

Fred   Ah. Don't worry, love, that's just a bit of a whiff from my petrol lighter.

Penelope Oh … !

Delia (*rising*) Excuse me.

Delia leaves the room. The others gaze after her.

Dudley   Again? … Well, what did you think of this red?

Penelope I think it has character.

Dudley   I agree. It has backbone.

Penelope … and charm.

Dudley   And a certain impudence. What did you think, Gloria?

Gloria   I don't know, really.

Dudley   Glad?

Glad   I thought it was very – ordinary.

Penelope I detected a suggestion of blackberry.

Dudley   Oh! I thought – plum. Did you detect anything, Fred?

Fred   Branston Pickle.

Penelope Ridiculous!

As they all look at Fred, Delia returns.

Gloria   You missed some very interesting comments, Delia.

Delia smiles wanly and sits.

Dudley   Ahem! … We must move on. We have yet to consider a *Chardonnay Merlot Vin de Pays de* Bletchley, a Stony Stratford lightly oaked white and a Lakes Estate Red, with one or two others in reserve …

His voice fades. A notice reading 'TWO HOURS LATER' is carried across the stage. While this is happening, more bottles have appeared on the table and the members of the group look distinctly the worse for wear.

Dudley   Ladies and gen'men – I wish to shay a few words (*murmurs of approval*) – about where we are. – Where are we? – Oh, yes, this meeting of the Wine appreshiashon Group is a truly memorall – memorabibble occasion. Why? – because we are on the threshold of a new year – a new censhury – and a new minellium – millellium – whatever – and next time we meet, it will no longer be 1999. It will be 2000.

Fred   Hear, hear!

Delia (*rising*) Excuse me.   (*She leaves the room. The others take no notice.*)

Dudley   … and when it's 2000, you must remember … you must remember … to pay your subs! – So, here's a toast – several toasts – to the New year! (*They drink.*) To the new censhury! (*They drink.*) To the New Minennium!

They drink again. Suddenly Glad sits bolt upright and begins to sing in a cracked voice.

Fred   Shurrup, Glad!

Dudley   Er – Fred … Glad has started singing.

Fred   Well – she always does.

Dudley   So, hadn't you better take her home?

Fred   No!

Dudley   Fred … !

Fred   Someone else can take her home.

Dudley   But, Fred …

Fred   I take her home every time. Why should it always be me?

Dudley   Well, you are her husband.

Fred   Yes – that's true, worse luck! (*He rises.*) Shurrup, Glad, time to go home. There's nothing left to drink. Come on.

Fred gets Glad to her feet. Suddenly Penelope stands up and begins to strip. The others watch for a moment.

Dudley   She doesn't usually do that so early in the afternoon.

Gloria takes charge, preventing further stripping.

Gloria   I'll get her home. Come on, Penelope, there's a good girl.

Dudley   Perhaps we'd better close the meeting.

Fred and Glad, Gloria and Penelope stagger out.

    I declare the meeting closed … .

Dudley falls asleep, his head on the table, as Delia enters. She looks round and rushes out.

CURTAIN OR BLACKOUT

Pip Parry, the late Pete Jones, and Cy Pearson, in costume for *Words, Words, Words* (see page 73).

A TAP performance of ***Keep out of reach of children*** (page 115): standing, Vera Roper as Mrs Dale; L to R: Jocelyn Lord as Jane; John Fone as Alvin; Thelma Billington as Mary; Christina Lay as Roberta.

The Editor, reading the Narration at the Third-Age Players' Christmas
Show of 2001.

Performing Rights Application Form

Please post to: *Parrilay Plays, c/o Pip Parry, 17 Lissel Road, Simpson, Milton Keynes. MK6*

Please enclose an A4 s.a.e. **or** a stamped label. Please reply to **all** questions. Attach a separate sheet if necessary.

Date of application ... ...

1   Name of applicant:

Dr / Ms / Mr ... ...

2   Application on behalf of (self or

organisation) ... ...

3   Return address, telephone No., **e-mail:**

... ...

... ...

4   Item(s) for which performance approval is sought

... ...

... ...

5   Does / do the item(s) need to be adapted for use in a

different geographical locality?   **Yes/No**

If so, please state area and / or attach a list of proposed changes.

... ...

... ...

6   Status of organisation (amateur or commercial theatre,

educational, charity ,etc) ... ...

Please continue overleaf

7   Venue(s), number, dates, and times of proposed
performance(s)

… …
… …
(Note that applications need to be received at least one month in advance of
first performance date.)

8   Approximate number of audience expected on each
occasion … … … … … … … … … … … … … … … … … … …

9   Proposed ticket or entry charge per person, and
beneficiary / ies

… …

10   Further relevant information

… …
… …

11   Signature … … … … … … … … … …

For office use only   **Application No. … … … …**

Date received … … … … discussed with (if nec) … … … … …

DECISION / Terms… … … … … … … …   **Total Fee due** … … … … …

Methods of sending decision… … … … … … … … … … … … …

Tick & initial when done   ☐ … … … …

Cheque received   ☐   cleared   ☐ … … … …

Review from Editor of *The Speaker*

The Association of Speakers Clubs

www.the-asc.org.uk

It was a pleasure and a privilege to be invited to review
Hidden Treasures. It was suggested that it might be just the thing for
members of the Association of Speakers Clubs to use on
Poetry Nights, or for exercises in voice projection – or even just for
that reading event which comes around every so often.

I chuckled my way through much of it and sighed my way through
parts of it. I smiled and enjoyed and read aloud those bits that were
just too good to be smothered to oneself.

Pip Parry is to be congratulated on producing some very fine material.
I am sure that it will be well received in Speakers Clubs and
Drama Groups, or just for sheer entertainment by the individual.

I wish all concerned with the book every success.

Irene Dick, BA, MSc
Editor, *The Speaker*,
(Journal of The Association of Speakers Clubs)